Praises for *"No Thank You, Mr. President"*

"When John Cohoat told me about his book at a recent talk in Elkhart County, I told him it's wonderful to hear from the people of Elkhart County and know that they are focused on their own recovery. John's book captures the spirit of small business in America today ... moving ahead despite all the road blocks our Government is trying to put in their way."

Mike Pence
Indiana Congressman

"John Cohoat did a great job in putting this book together and it is a real testament how Entrepreneurs can not only survive, but THRIVE in tough economic times. Every business owner should read this book and will be inspired to overcome any adversity that they might experience."

Bill Glazer
President, Glazer-Kennedy Insider's Circle™
The PLACE For PROSPERITY™

"As a residential developer in Central Indiana, we've been hit hard by the downturn and I can tell you that sometimes it's hard to find silver linings in the Recession Clouds. "No Thank You, Mr. President" makes me remember why our company fights the fight every day and gives me hope that all of us will come back. Thanks, John."

Paul Estridge, President
The Estridge Companies
Featured in ABC's Extreme Makeover, 2009 Season Finale

"Being an Elkhart county small business owner myself with clients as far away as New Zealand and who's business grew even during the recession, I'm so glad that John Cohoat took time out of his busy life to interview and tell 'the rest of the Elkhart County story'. Bailouts and handouts are not the answer and John nailed that message. This is an inspiring book full of stories of rising above the mediocre crowd. You won't want to put it down."

Nina Hershberger
www.MegabucksMarketing.com

"I really appreciate the effort it takes as a first time author, because I went through this the last year with my own book. John has done a masterful job finding great stories from our friends in Northern Indiana and has a put a unique spotlight on the entrepreneurial spirit."

David A. Bego, President, Executive Management Services, Inc. and author, "The Devil at My Doorstep"

"John Cohoat's book highlights many of the same concerns we all have about where our government is going and how it is failing us. However, John recounts how capitalism and Midwest values can still be the beacon of hope for our great Country. As a farmer, author and small business owner, I can tell you this book really resonates with me and I highly recommend you read it soon to rekindle your spirit."

Bill Shuttleworth, President, Shuttleworth Insurance
and author, "The 2nd American Revolution"

No Thank You, Mr. President

How Real Businesses from Elkhart County, Indiana Stood Up to Fight and Thrive on Their Own in Spite of the Economic Turmoil

By John S. Cohoat

Foreword by Lou Holtz

With an Introduction and Special Chapter from Dan S. Kennedy

An Imprint of Morgan James Publishing

No Thank You, Mr. President

How Real Businesses from Elkhart County, Indiana Stood Up to Fight and Thrive On Their Own in Spite of the Economic Turmoil

ISBN 978-0-98237-935-6

Library of Congress Control Number: 2009941943

Glazer-Kennedy publishing

Imprint of:
Morgan James Publishing
1225 Franklin Ave., STE 325
Garden City, NY 11530-1693
Toll Free 800-485-4943
www.MorganJamesPublishing.com

Contents

Foreword

Many know me as a former football coach at the University of Notre Dame and the years I was there were some of the best of my life. During this time I was proud to be a Hoosier from the great State of Indiana. The county next to the one we lived in was Elkhart County, Indiana, which for decades has been known as the Recreational Vehicle Capital of the World. I may not be the smartest guy in the world, but I know that when the gas crisis, credit crunch and economic downturn hit our Country at the same time, we were all affected, but nowhere quite as hard as Elkhart County, which now experienced one of the highest unemployment rates in the Nation, nearly 20%. When I read about this, I was saddened because I had gotten to know many people from that area who were great supporters of Notre Dame and astute businesspeople.

As I watched the press coverage of the situation in Elkhart County I was very concerned about how the area was portrayed by national media, as if the only way to come back was with massive assistance from the Federal Government. Many spending and so-called reform policies of the Obama Administration can actually have the effect of making it much more difficult for our States, businesses and families to prosper and to recover on our own. And, from what I know of people in Elkhart County, they will not be looking for someone to bail them out. I know they will work through this situation as they have before when challenges have hit the area.

John Cohoat's new book tells a story I know to be true, because I have visited Elkhart County and have friends from there. I am pleased that John has focused on the Midwest values of taking care of our own and rugged responsibility for our own recovery. With all the discussion in our Nation about what is the proper role of government, this book puts it all in perspective. These businesses and the people who work there are the real heroes in our Country and I'm pleased that you can learn more about them in this wonderful book.

Lou Holtz
ESPN Analyst and Former Hoosier

(Lou Holtz is widely regarded as one of the most successful college football coaches of all time. He compiled a 243–127–7 career record and was inducted into the College Football Hall of Fame in 2008. During 11 seasons at Notre Dame, Holtz posted a 100–30–2 record that included a national championship in 1988. Lou currently serves as a college football studio analyst on ESPN. He is also the author of six books, including best sellers The Fighting Spirit; Winning Everyday: A Game Plan for Success; and Wins, Losses and Lessons. He is a highly sought-after speaker on the subject of overcoming seemingly impossible challenges by setting your own goals and working to achieve them. In 2009 Lou has also appeared on national news shows discussing current political and economic issues.)

Introduction

When John Cohoat approached me about his new book, the topic grabbed me, because I was well aware of the problems in Elkhart County Indiana and the rest of our Country. I live just a few hours east of Elkhart County and had noticed the problems of the Recreational Vehicle (RV) Industry, especially with all the sensational coverage by the Liberal Media. Like John, I was disturbed seeing President Obama staging events in Elkhart to tell them and all Americans why his Stimulus Plan was the answer to their woes.

In my 30 plus years of working with tens of thousands of businesses, I've never found one whose success strategy was to rely on any governmental entity for its sales and profits.

John contacted me early on in his writing process and I encouraged him to move forward quickly. And, he did. I knew he had recently become an Independent Business Advisor with Glazer-Kennedy Insider's Circle (my main business) and there is a tremendous amount of work and training to get his local chapter started. But, frankly, I thought the need to tell the story of Elkhart County entrepreneurs was even more important. We don't need more people sticking their hands out looking for someone to bail them out. Many of our politicians offer all kinds of assistance and essentially paralyze some of our fellow citizens who think there is nothing to do but wait for the State or Federal government to come to their rescue. This thinking is dangerous, because there is no way such a strategy is sustainable, at least with the lifestyle and opportunity we have been used to in our United States.

In the last several months, John has successfully recruited members for his chapter, while at the same time interviewing the companies featured in this book and writing their stories. As a first time author, John has done a masterful job. A Midwest guy myself, I can tell you John has captured the essence of Midwest entrepreneurial spirit. I didn't personally know any of these companies before I read John's book, but now I feel a real connection, much as I do with many of my clients who share the same values and hard working mentality. I'd love to work with the businesses featured in this book because they display the "can do" approach that I look for in my clients.

What we teach at Glazer-Kennedy is really blocking and tackling of marketing and business strategy. There is nothing overly complicated about what our thousands of members do....it's just that they're willing to learn, master and implement. So, while many of the stories in this book are fascinating and the challenges faced have been huge, the stories are universal and repeated all across the United States (with the possible exception of California. I have no idea what's going on there.)

The point is we need to be reminded of these stories and realize that small businesses and people rolling up their sleeves every day are what really matters. Government never really helps. They just get in the way and make the entrepreneur's job that much tougher by taxing them, regulating them and interfering in their free markets. How we get our politicians to realize this is the challenge of our generation.

The theme of this book is not so much a repudiation of the socialist policies of the current Obama Administration, but rather evidence why the capitalist economic system really works. And, it works even in tough times, because the basic good in each individual, a desire to succeed and ingenuity are the formulas for success. This is the way we've been approaching the Recession with our members. Our 2009 SuperConference had the theme "Recession Rescue" and I've been giving my observations about how to respond to the Recession in our newsletters, weekly faxes and many speeches this year. John has been paying attention and asked if he could compile some of my thoughts into a special report as a bonus for his book.

So, chapter 14 is just that. There is a collection of my essays, articles, speaking notes and more that has been gathered together for your review. You already have some great examples from the companies in this book, but I'm pleased to share some of my thoughts. We realize that the current economic situation has affected us all….I've adjusted my approach, lost a few clients, but gained some others. We changed some things at Glazer-Kennedy Insider's Circle. Know that we have continued to grow and our conferences still are setting records while many business conferences have been canceled or had dramatic drops in attendance. Many of our members are having banner years, because of good marketing, sound strategy and a willingness to plow forward when everyone else is sitting on the sidelines. My hope is that John's book and this information from me will reinforce what you are already doing or shift your mindset if you have settled for waiting out the Recession. Opportunity is still all around us. You just need to find it.

As you dive into this book, prepare to be inspired and to remember what is great about our Country. Do what you can in your personal lives and local businesses to fight on in tough times. And, get involved with the political process, so our leaders know what you are about and, if they don't get it, vote them out.

Dan S. Kennedy

(*Dan Kennedy is a serial entrepreneur, adviser to business owners, sought-after speaker and author of 13 books. He writes a weekly political commentary for the Business and Media Institute, www.businessandmedia.org. More information about Dan can be found at www.NoBSBooks.com, and a free collection of his business resources including newsletters and webinars at www.DanKennedy.com.)*

1) Why This Book? Why Now?

January 14, 2009 was an eventful day in the Cohoat family. Early in the morning I took off for Indianapolis in a blizzard for three days of meetings and some planning with my boss. On the way he called me to say, "Don't come. The roads are too bad. Oh, and by the way, times are tough in real estate development, and your position has been eliminated effective two days from now. Sorry." So I turned around and headed for home. "Wonder how to tell my wife, Adrienne? She's just been getting used to me having this nice pay check."

When I got home, I called her to let her know I wouldn't be gone the next few nights. I'd deliver the bad news in person tonight. But she wasn't at the office, and her co-worker asked me if I'd heard from her. "No," I said. Well, she'd been in a car accident. She was OK, but she wasn't there yet. I called her cell phone frantically, but there was no answer. After about an hour she called me. She'd flipped over our little four-wheel-drive truck on the Indiana Toll Road and just missed a tree sliding off. She landed upside-down in a ditch. The truck was totaled, but with the exception of a few bumps and bruises, she was fine. I told her I'd come get her, but she didn't want me on the roads because they were too dangerous.

That night she came home with one of her co-workers, and we hugged and told each other how much we loved the other. After a few minutes, I told her my news. Given her brush with death, it didn't seem so bad. I told her there was a decent severance package and we'd figure it out. Besides, we had just sold our business, The Patchwork Quilt Country Inn, and we were slated to close on the deal on February 3. Some of our financial obligations were going away.

As I honestly assessed the situation, I knew this was an opportunity to remake my career. While I'd take a look at some nice job options over the next few months, my heart was in doing something on my own. I had remained a member of Glazer Kennedy Insider's Circle (GKIC) during my tenure at the big public real estate company, and that's the direction I saw myself going—some kind of business I could run by myself. Eventually I invested virtually all of my severance in the purchase of a territory and arrangement with GKIC where I would become the local GKIC Certified No B.S. Business Advisor for Northern Indiana and Southwest Michigan. I would run my own chapter and work with local entrepreneurs, small businesses, and sales professionals to show them how to increase their sales and profits using GKIC-style marketing. It was very exciting for me—not so much for Adrienne.

The week after I lost my job was President Barack Obama's inauguration. I hadn't been happy about how things were going with the Bush administration, but I'm definitely a conservative. I was not happy that the Republicans chose John McCain, who turned out to be a very weak candidate. And I was not at all pleased by what I'd heard from Obama, but maybe—just maybe—he could bring us together. Maybe he wouldn't be so bad.

Right away any real hope was dashed as we found out about the Massive Stimulus Bill. And guess what? Obama was making my county, Elkhart County, Indiana, the poster child for all that is bad with our economy. He was coming back in early February to tell us how he was going to bail us out with all this spending—as if we couldn't do it ourselves.

Over the years, I'd had a multi-faceted business career. Upon graduating from Notre Dame with an accounting degree in 1976, I took the traditional route and worked for a huge international accounting firm. After eight successful years, I took a job with a small company in Pittsburgh as its first CFO, with stock ownership given to me. We were very entrepreneurial, and it was a lot of fun. The CEO thought the company was his own private checkbook, so when some shareholders came after him, I thought I'd get out, since he had no intention of changing his ways. I made a nice chunk of change when they had to buy back my stock.

At age thirty-two I moved back to South Bend to become the CEO at a small hospital. I had never even worked for a hospital, but now I was running one, plus several small clinics and side businesses. My career was really taking off, and I managed a nice financial turnaround for the hospital, did a great strategic plan, made some key management changes, and started to make a name for myself.

So then in 1990, I bought Bonnie Doon Ice Cream, a fifty-year-old family ice cream company with drive-in restaurants and a very small ice cream plant. When my partner felt like he needed more help to run it, I quit my hospital CEO job, took a big pay cut, and ran Bonnie Doon for several years. We found the restaurant business challenging but tried our best. Most of the restaurants were sold to provide capital or repay debt. The wholesale production and distribution of ice cream was an opportunity, so we bought a 26,000 square foot former Indiana Toll Road commissary building in Elkhart and moved our production there. All of a sudden, we had three or four trucks on the road every day, and we had hundreds of wholesale accounts. We grew the wholesale business from a few thousand dollars to more than $2 million in a few years. The business was tough, margins were thin, and we could never really achieve what we wanted in terms of profits and cash flow. The bank noticed this and became a vocal, threatening critic.

Through a series of volunteer activities and some networking, I was offered an opportunity to return to healthcare with a nice officer position at Holy Cross Health System, based in South Bend. In 1998, I went back into the big company atmosphere. Taking my salary off the Bonnie Doon payroll provided more cash for my partner and took some pressure off from the banks. Eventually we got some new partners, and I sold my interest in 2001.

We had a few years of relative stability. Holy Cross was a nice place to work. The salary was good and stable. The job was fine, but many times I had to bite my tongue as I observed the politics and weird decision-making in a religious organization. Again, opportunity presented itself when the Sisters decided to sell us to a larger Catholic healthcare system in Detroit. Our corporate office was closed, and we didn't think we'd like moving up to Detroit, so I took the generous severance and went on my way.

With the severance money and the sale of Bonnie Doon, I had a little money. So Adrienne and I moved from the typical suburban lifestyle outside South Bend to the small town of Middlebury and eighteen acres in the country. We purchased the Patchwork Quilt Country Inn, with fifteen guest rooms and a hundred-seat country dining restaurant. It was a nice lifestyle for a few years—great guests, paid the bills, but not a get-rich-quick scheme. And managing the whole thing started to become a problem.

So again, I was drawn back to a big company when my brother, who was the CFO, told me they had a new healthcare development company and were looking for people like me. My network in healthcare and executive experience was a nice fit for healthcare real estate business development. Everything was going pretty well until the housing bubble burst, the credit crunch happened, and the stock market crashed. The company got very risk averse, and they decided to start shutting down development and wait this thing out. My job was eliminated since there was no need for business development, which got us to January 14.

So when Obama brought his hope and change to Concord High School, I wasn't impressed. I knew I wasn't interested in his handouts. I'd figure something out like I always had. "No thank you, Mr. President. We can do it on our own like we always have." And I knew many entrepreneurs and business leaders in Elkhart County felt the same way. The real story of our entrepreneurial community and how we were coming back on our own needed to be told. And I decided to tell it.

This book is about ordinary businesspeople doing extraordinary things every day. Some of the companies I knew about. Others I was told about when I started inquiring about who was working hard, coming back, and succeeding despite all the negativity and tough economic times.

And I have to say, there are hundreds more businesses in our area which could be in this book—and thousands across the country. My hope is that these stories provide some inspiration for you or make you remember why our capitalist economic policies and truly American way of life is the answer. All of it seems under assault right now, so this may inspire you to get involved. Or it may make you understand entrepreneurs and small business better. Or it might make you rededicate yourself to your own business or find a new venture that excites you. In my mind, this is the real type of hope we need right now.

2) Prepared for Change

Mapletronics Computers

Things may be tough in Elkhart County right now, but Wes Hershberger and Mapletronics Computers have built their business around responding to disasters and change for many years. They've lived it all—flooded offices, Y2K, 9/11, Katrina, major growth issues, a few bad profit years, banks pulling out the rugs, etc. And through it all, the attitude has been, "we will just forge on"—and in fact, they've used what they learned and observed to make their business stronger. They now use that ability to make their customers' lives easier, so they can be prepared for change, too.

Mapletronics was really born in 1992 when Wes and his wife, Janelle, bought an existing company, T&C Electronics. T&C's primary business was a Radio Shack dealership. Wes had built some computers himself and wanted to expand his presence in the local market by offering those computers through T&C. The name of the company was quickly changed to Mapletronics (their home city is Goshen, Indiana, known as the Maple City). By 1995, the Radio Shack dealership was sold.

Over the next several years, the company focused on building high-quality computers, competing with Gateway, Dell, HP, IBM, and anyone else willing to buy a bunch of components, assemble them, and sell you a computer. Mapletronics has always concentrated on building much higher quality computers, using primarily American-made components with only the best suppliers. The computers are built in such a fashion that they can be easily serviced by Mapletronics techs. And the price has always been higher than the bargain offerings from competitors. One of Wes's major tenets was starting to show its face—never compete on price, and don't be in a commodity business.

Wes is a planner and visionary. He had aggressive growth goals and plans. By 1997, after only five years, the company had met its ten-year sales goals and was ready to embark on a new ten-year plan. The year 1997 had been explosive, with sales growth of 96 percent. Wes was having trouble managing all this growth. The company needed new facilities and more people. A new growth plan was developed, but to Wes it seemed like more of the same, and it was starting to feel like his PCs were just a commodity, largely competing on price.

So he told everyone they were scrapping the plan. They would find other ways to grow. They had started to do some training, so that became a major component—one that would come in very handy in 2008. But while hardware sales were the vast majority of the business, Wes wanted to move to a service orientation.

As most of us know, usually from some catastrophe or problem in our own offices, data can easily be lost, resulting in downtime and much cost to restore or rebuild records. Wes was aware of this and took measured precautions in his own business, probably much more than the average company using networks and PCs. When he received a call from his alarm company on a stormy night in 1998, he thought it was probably just a false alarm. He arrived at his building to find that the water was pouring into his offices and server rooms faster than it was raining outside. A portion of the metal roof had been blown back by the storm in such a way that the water was coming in torrents through the drop ceilings.

He called his key people, who showed up at 6:00 AM. For the next several days they cleaned up. But they had contingency plans and backups of servers and data. The main server was back by 10:00 AM the same day, and despite some damage to a few customer computers which were in for repair and other water damage, the business was basically back in operation right away. They even sold a few computers that day.

One of the main service lines of Mapletronics today is Data Protection Services. About nine years ago, Wes decided that the future of this type of service was through the Internet. Most companies were still struggling with tape backup systems, but Wes recognized that technology allowed an Internet data transfer and backup approach.

Today we all hear about Web-based backups for home and small business systems. Mapletronics has systems to back up entire networks. Wes and his sales staff provide the customer with an analysis of the types of disasters which can strike and ask them what level of assurance they want. How long can they be down? What level of data loss since the last backup is acceptable? The systems are then designed to provide what the customer can live with. It's very much a value sell.

In 2006, Wes wrote a book entitled *When IT Hits the Fan.* The first part of the book is a fictional account of a mid-sized company experiencing a data disaster, as well as struggling with the value of their investment in information technology. The second part of the book ties various strategic options to the fictional account and becomes a primer on how CEOs and IT executives need to approach the planning and management of their IT. Wes self-published the book and even formed a small publishing company to do that. He hopes to publish a few more books.

Wes has leveraged off this book to create instant credibility with his clients and potential customers. He also offers several free seminars on similar topics to get customers thinking about the need for his services. Service has now become more than 80 percent of the company's business, so the plan that Wes implemented in the late '90s has been realized.

Mapletronics stresses a management services approach to IT. Their goal is to analyze the client's IT needs in concert with the client. Then a monthly management agreement is crafted, with ongoing payments. Both the client and Mapletronics take some risk in this arrangement, but Wes believes it creates a true partnership with the customer. When customers and their staff have simple tech questions they are encouraged to call their dedicated Mapletronics staff, who will help them through the answer. This adds much value to the relationship and saves the client time and money. Wes's belief is that the big technology companies such as IBM and Dell may be able to grow and add services, but they can never duplicate the relationship Wes has with his clients.

Twice, bank relationships have put Wes and his company in very difficult positions. Despite the issues with Y2K and September 11, the company was enjoying great growth and success; plus Wes had his long-term vision of an even better, larger company. So he needed a bigger facility. They purchased a building in Goshen and began construction in late 2000. Everything was going fine until they realized they were $500,000 over budget, a surprise not welcomed by their bank at the time. The profit situation had softened a little (the company has only had two loss years in its history). So the bank wouldn't provide the final financing for the building. Mapletronics couldn't stay in its present facility and couldn't move into its new one.

As the true entrepreneur, Wes was able to convince another bank that they should fund him. Wes had seen no real way out of that mess, but he saw a Divine hand in what happened. Because of multiple delays, he actually got a much lower interest rate, saving the company more than $100,000. Several times, when describing some of the tough situations or disasters they have come through, Wes made reference to the fact that he's a man of faith, and this faith runs through his philosophy of running his company and how he treats his sixty-plus employees. The philosophy of service to his customers is embodied in the company slogan, *Improving Lives through Technology*, which Wes sees as almost a spiritual calling.

As a side note, just last year, the bank that showed faith in Wes in the early 2000s pulled the plug. When growth and profits reached a plateau in 2007, the bank became uncomfortable. Through the many relationships Wes had in the community, a local bank stepped in, and Wes feels that the company has a solid relationship with the bank. The year 2008 was a record sales year, and profits were at a good level; 2009 is holding up for a slight growth, so the stage is set for Wes's next ten-year plan. His goal is to be at $100 million in sales by 2017, which would be dramatic growth as they are currently just under $9 million annualized for 2009.

Of the businesses interviewed for this book, Mapletronics may be the one that is best trying to capitalize on the current economic situation. As mentioned, they started training services several years ago as a way to attract potential clients, add value for their clients, and increase the supply of qualified technicians. With the recent decline of the RV industry, there are many displaced workers looking for a change of career. Wes and his team have applied to the State of Indiana for training grants to the tune of more than $1 million. This has been a profitable part of their business and has allowed them to continue to grow despite the local economy.

Wes appears undeterred about the current economic conditions. He has no intention of reducing his growth plans. Mapletronics branches have opened operations in Fort Wayne, Indiana and Sarasota, Florida and continue to look for regional opportunities to expand, perhaps by acquisition of companies with similar services in new geographic locations. Other lines of business are constantly being evaluated.

Here's just a partial list of the services now provided by Mapletronics:

- Custom-built computers and servers (the original business)
- Network design and engineering
- Web hosting
- Mapletronics Internet services
- Various training in hardware and software
- Data Protection Planning and services
- IT management services contracts
- Home and office showroom with typical computer supplies, cables, etc.

These multiple streams of income contribute to the stability of the company and provide clients a one-stop shop, if so desired. Wes mentioned a concern that they haven't done a great job of letting all their customers know all that they could do for them. So this is potential growth opportunity. Some of these services have been developed in-house, while others have been added by the acquisition of small companies with complementary services or geographic reach. Wes believes he has built his company for growth and will continue to explore these options in the future.

Another area of strength is the vertical diversity of their industries served. Mapletronics has many small manufacturers and other businesses in their core market who are suffering from the dramatic recession in the area. However, growing vertical markets include health care and K-12 education. Both markets are providing nice growth for the company.

As a further example of how Wes and his team approach their markets, they have recently implemented a new service to their education clients in Indiana. They hired a recognized consultant from the industry with the express purpose of showing Indiana schools how to use money from the Stimulus package. While this apparently has no relation to the core business of Mapletronics, this service further enhances the relationship with education clients and could provide an entry to some schools that aren't currently using the company's services. Besides, Wes is convinced that technology will be an answer as to how to best spend much of the Stimulus money, and he is poised to take advantage when that route is chosen. This is truly an innovative marketing approach and shows Wes's ability to step outside industry norms.

Intel has recognized the innovation, quality, and sales abilities of Mapletronics and has appointed Wes to their National Board of Advisors. This relationship enhances Wes's credibility, taps him in to industry leaders, and provides advance notice of major product announcements by Intel.

As Wes and I talked about the current situation in Elkhart County, he was hesitant to blame current political leaders in the area. His view was that the county should have capitalized on its strength, so reliance on the RV industry made good sense. He generally believes that the new crop of elected officials who will represent the county at the state level are approachable and smart, while also sharing many of his Christian values. They haven't had much time in office, and Wes hopes they can represent the county well. As a fiscal and social conservative, Wes is also generally in tune with the agenda of Indiana Governor Mitch Daniels, although he wonders whether some educational budget cuts go too far—at the expense of our children's futures. On a national basis, Wes shares the concern of many that the massive spending and takeover of industries spells economic disaster.

His comments about this were enlightening. I asked, "What if all of this leads to financial Armageddon?"

Wes responded in a typical fashion, given his seventeen-year track record. "Well, we will find out what the new rules are after the Armageddon and get on with it." There's no quit here and no sense that Mapletronics won't still be successful for years to come.

MAPLETRONICS COMPUTERS

KEYS TO SUCCESS:

- Have a vision and an aggressive plan.
- Commit to your plan—no matter what.
- Also, have a plan for disaster.
- Don't let your products or services become a commodity.
- Focus on the customer, and build a partnership with them.
- Manage and lead around your core spiritual values.
- Look for multiple streams of income.
- Find out what the new rules are, and adapt.
- Take advantage of the new rules, even if you don't agree with all of them.
- Be resilient.

Contact information if you want to know more about Mapletronics Computers or contact Wes:

Mapletronics Computers
3116 W. Wilden Ave.
P.O. Box 136
Goshen, IN 46527-0136
Phone: 574.534.2830
Toll Free: 800.358.7447
Fax: 574.534.2730
www.mapletronics.com
Wes Hershberger, CEO
E-mail: whersch@emaple.net

3) RV Industry Leader Grabbing Market Share in Tough Times

Jayco, Inc.

As I considered the companies to include in this book, I wondered whether any RV companies would be good candidates. The industry has been decimated the last few years. To put it all in perspective, in 1978 RV shipments totaled almost 400,000 nationwide. By 1980, shipments were down to nearly 100,000, with almost 75 percent of the business gone. Since then, the industry has steadily increased most years, with the exception of some tough times in 1989-1991, when each year was off in the 5-10 percent range, and a downward blip in 2001 with September 11. In 2006, the industry finally got back up where it had been in 1978, hitting 390,000 total units shipped. In 2007, they were off 9.5 percent; in 2008, down 33 percent; and 2009 is projected to be off by 45 percent. As the RV Capital of the World, the Elkhart county region has also grown in percentage of total RVs shipped from around 45 percent twenty years ago to around 60 percent now. In short, Elkhart County's local economy and the RV business are in lock step.

As I spoke with business leaders and asked them who really had a pulse on what was happening, they told me I should talk to Wilbur Bontrager, chairperson of Jayco. I already knew Wilbur from chamber of commerce events, having helped out with our town's local economic development committee, chaired by Wilbur.

Jayco truly is a leader in the RV industry and a well-known name throughout the country. The company was founded by Lloyd Bontrager, Wilbur's father, in 1968. Lloyd had been raised Amish and had worked in the local Starcraft plant for many years, having decided to become Mennonite. He believed he knew a way to build a better pop-up camper, so he got together a plan and started production in converted farm buildings with some local Amish and Mennonite workers. The first year they produced 132 campers, and in the second year this rose to more than one thousand. Lloyd's wife, Bertha, was the office manager, operating out of a small room in the main farmhouse while she cared for her children.

The company quickly got a reputation for the quality of its products and honesty in dealing with the customers. Dealers came on at a rapid pace, and growth was explosive. Jayco started making other types of RVs, including towables, fifth wheels, park model trailers, and eventually motorized RVs, so that they had a full product line.

The first crisis to hit the company happened in 1972. Lloyd had taken up flying, and Jayco had a plant in Kansas. In March of 1972, Lloyd and Freeman Miller, a twenty-year-old Amish line foreman, went for a plant visit. Freeman was along primarily as company for Lloyd, and although the Amish typically don't fly, Freeman had decided to go along. No one is sure what happened—perhaps a fueling error by the airport they stopped at to refuel—but for whatever reason, Lloyd had to ditch the plane in a Kansas wheat field, and Freeman was killed while Lloyd was critically injured. Lloyd recovered over the next few months, taking many phone calls and visitors in his hospital room to keep things going. One of his roommates eventually became one of Jayco's top sales executives.

Sales topped $10 million in 1972—no small feat for a four-year-old company. Now the first financial crisis came upon them as the Arab Oil Embargo reared its head in 1973. Jayco was able to weather this storm for a while by growing its dealer network, and they also had started producing a line of boats. Industry unit production declined almost 40 percent in 1974 to just under 300,000 units, and Jayco was feeling it. Lloyd had to start laying off employees, close plants in Kansas and Canada, and initiate management pay cuts or give IOUs just to survive. As a relatively new company, capital to survive was hard to come by. Lloyd was able to arrange a loan with St. Joseph Valley Bank, but one condition was that all upper management had to personally guarantee the debt. Most were not shareholders, so this was a very tough sales job for Lloyd; but they all believed in him, and the deal was done.

As the industry and Jayco recovered in the '70s, they began expansion into Australia, along with continued growth in dealers and unit sales in the U. S. and Canada. As the huge 1979 and 1980 crunches hit, Jayco was more prepared financially, and despite the need to lay off employees and downsize, survivability never seemed to be an issue. While many other companies were shutting down, Jayco was actually introducing lightweight, energy-efficient product lines and capturing much more market share. In 1980, Jayco entered the European market with a joint venture arrangement.

As the industry recovered in the early '80s, Jayco continued to assert itself in the market, expanding product offerings and building its dealer network. In 1985, lightning struck with even more fury. Lloyd, his sixteen-year-old son Wendall, Nelson Hershberger (a Jayco R&D executive), and Marshall, Nelson's seventeen-year-old son had traveled to Florida in Lloyd's plane for a week of fun combined with a little business. On Easter Sunday morning, they flew through a strong spring storm and crashed in Muncie, Indiana. All four were killed. The tragic loss of company leaders and young men devastated the families and the community. Jayco employees wondered how the company would function without their visionary leader, Lloyd, who was so identified with Jayco.

Lloyd's sons, Wilbur and Derald, worked in the business, but were still very early in their business careers. Fortuitously, Lloyd had brought in a seasoned banker, Al Yoder, who was the chief operating officer at the time of Lloyd's death. Al became the CEO and was able to provide stability. Bertha Bontrager also came back into the company as chairperson to continue her husband's legacy.

Al was well known in Jayco circles, and the company really didn't miss a beat. Another recession hit in 1989 and 1990, with dramatic declines in the RV industry again. With all Jayco had been through in earlier downturns, plus the other crises, they just pulled out the old playbooks and kept moving forward. Starcraft, one of Jayco's strongest competitors and the company Lloyd had worked at before he founded Jayco, went bankrupt in 1990. Jayco bought Starcraft out of bankruptcy and continues to produce this line of RVs today.

From 1983 to 1993, Jayco doubled in size, and Al Yoder groomed new management to take over when he retired in 1993. Bernie Lambright, who had been a consultant and executive at Jayco for many years, became CEO, while Wilbur became chairperson, and Derald became executive vice president, replacing Wilbur in this role. Bertha became chairperson emeritus. The final transition to full Bontrager management occurred in 2002 when Bernie retired and Wilbur added the title of CEO, while Derald became president and COO.

Today Jayco is the largest privately owned RV Company in the world and is headquartered in the tiny town of Middlebury, Indiana.

So what is the situation at one of the nation's top RV companies today? I met with Wilbur Bontrager in the late summer of 2009, and he recounted where the company has been. Sales have fallen dramatically from a yearly high of about $750 million to a projection of just over $300 million in 2009. Unit volume is off from about 30,000 annually to approximately 17,000 for 2009. The sales are down more on a percentage basis as the higher-priced, motorized

RVs have recorded more dramatic drops (more than 70 percent) than campers and trailers because of gas prices. Jayco's products sell for anywhere from $6,000 for a tent camper to $450,000 for a luxury RV. As you can imagine, profit margins are higher for upper-end models, so profits have declined. Wilbur states that monthly profitability has returned during the summer and for 2009 year-to-date; but the year will be touch and go as the last few months are always lower profit months in the RV industry.

Employment is similarly off, and this has been the toughest situation to deal with. Several plants have been closed and production of various models consolidated. Total employment peaked at 2,400 after Jayco purchased some assets and a line of luxury RVs from Travel Supreme, which had gone into bankruptcy a few years ago. It fell to less than 1,200 in early 2009. About 150 employees have been called back, but Wilbur is concerned that the coming fall and winter will be very tight.

While the industry unit volume has been off by about 40 percent, Jayco has "only" been off 30 percent, which means market share has increased by about 2.5 percent, and they are now in the 14 percent total market share range. They went into this downturn as the fourth-largest RV Company and now are a solid third. From a review of the company history and discussions with Wilbur, it appears this has happened in every downturn for the industry. The cream rises to the top, and poor competitors go away in recessions.

Wilbur has a firm grasp on the factors he believes have made Jayco a leader in the RV industry. First, the company was built on manufacturing excellence when Lloyd felt he could build a better camping trailer. All of the company's leaders have embraced the pursuit of quality, and this remains a key strength. The company is vertically integrated with plants or internal divisions producing virtually all furniture, upholstery, drapes, wiring harnesses, metal fabrication, trailers, lift systems, and more. Wilbur himself has a strong engineering background and started a company with his father several years ago, L&W Engineering, which still makes components for Jayco. Wilbur says that most RV companies purchase many of the components that Jayco produces for itself, so they retain the profit margins and also control the quality. This strategy is constantly examined and is even more in question during a downturn, since overhead is harder to cut when several hundred employees and many plants are involved in this vertical integration strategy. But Wilbur says they envision no changes to this strategy.

This product quality is given even more credence by their industry leading warranty program. Called the "Co-Pilot Warranty," each Jayco RV is under warranty for two years or 24,000 miles—compared to an industry standard of one year. Wilbur says this becomes a huge selling point and reinforces a premium pricing strategy. While they have many lines of products in various price ranges, the strategy has been to add value, rather than reduce price to compete, with examples of value being a free roadside assistance program and a travel club for Jayco owners. Wilbur mentions industry statistics which show that Jayco products move faster in dealer showrooms and also that used Jayco RVs have the best resale value in the business.

The strong Jayco dealer network is another key factor. Lloyd provided the example as he drove and flew the country getting to know dealers personally. Jayco has many dealer training programs, a dealer advisory board, and several incentives for being a Jayco dealer. There are more than 300 dealers in the U.S. with around eighty-five being exclusive to Jayco products. The company even provides architectural and construction consulting for dealers who want to upgrade or build a showroom with a Jayco look. Wilbur believes the dealer relationship with the consumer contributes greatly to customer satisfaction and eventual re-purchase of a Jayco product. In the era of online sales, RVs are now sold via the Internet, much like cars. However, Jayco requires that all Internet sales made by the customer have the product delivered by a trained, local dealer. While Jayco understands this may reduce some quick buck sales, they are willing to forego these sales to ensure a good dealer relationship and proper product delivery.

I believe the company's relatively conservative financial strategy has also served it well. While the RV industry goes through many boom times, it is subject to cyclical downturns. Jayco has chosen to invest in manufacturing and quality, plus a strong dealer network. However, they have resisted the temptation to own their dealers. At a time when financing has become a key issue for RV sales, Jayco has been approached to start its own finance company or joint venture with other players in this arena, like a GMAC or Ford Motor Credit for the RV industry. At this point, Wilbur says that is not a risk they want to take. While the company has some debt, it is not highly leveraged. For the most part, capital is internally generated, allowing them to withstand the tough times. And the company is owned by the Bontrager family, so they don't have to disclose their financial results or try to appeal to Wall Street analysts.

Looking forward, Wilbur is hopeful that the worst is behind us, although he doesn't believe good times will be here soon. He sees a tough next year or so. The word is that dealers have one to two years' supply of RV products in their inventories, meaning that orders will be slow—plus financing is still very tough for consumers and the RV dealers. While Wilbur agrees that there were many bad financing decisions over the last few years, he believes the pendulum has swung the other way and truly good credit consumers and dealers sometimes can't get financing. He is frustrated that all the stimulus and bailout talks have not really trickled to the RV industry, although local, state, and federal legislators have been going to bat for the industry.

Wilbur and Derald have been active in local and regional economic development efforts. Wilbur believes Elkhart County has good and well-intentioned leadership who are attempting to diversify its base. But Wilbur isn't so quick to throw out the baby with the bath water. He points out that the county has a strong base of factories and employees who know how to do what they do best. The type of manufacturing the county does is relatively unskilled and low capital intensive as compared to the auto industry, for example. The county has a strong supplier base, and transportation is relatively easy with access to major population bases.

Wilbur was really the first person to opine that we may see this area even more concentrated in the RV industry and like production. Many of the bigger players are actually consolidating headquarters and production in Indiana because of low costs of production, availability of space, good labor supply, and reduced transportation costs.

Wilbur rankles at the way Elkhart County has been portrayed, saying it has received much more attention than it should have. As the CEO of an entrepreneurial company, he is convinced it is a self-sufficient area which will come back on its own. His concern is that many policies of the Obama administration, like nationalized healthcare or proliferation of unions, may have permanent, harmful effects on how this county does business. Wilbur knows many local government officials and stays somewhat involved in political discussions. He went out of his way to mention the masterful job of Indiana governor Mitch Daniels, who has restored our state's fiscal reserves and seems to understand the plight of businesses. Personally, he has been exposed to other politicians years ago who had a priority of grabbing power and feathering their own nests, and he finds this very repugnant, so he is reluctant to get more involved politically.

Several years ago, two major RV companies were started in the Middlebury area. One was Coachmen, a fantastic company which eventually became public and just last year sold its entire RV business to a competitor in an effort to survive. The other is Jayco, which has remained independent and family owned, carrying on the legacy and vision of its founder, Lloyd Bontrager. As noted elsewhere in this book, the challenge for some family companies seems to come when the next generation of leadership doesn't embrace the founding principles of the company, either because the family is no longer involved or because others have taken over. Through unbelievable crises, Jayco has produced leaders both from outside and within the Bontrager family who have understood fundamental Jayco strategies that require consistent application, even in tough times. I believe Middlebury and Elkhart County can take solace in the fact that the Bontrager family is firmly committed to Jayco and its community.

Jayco, Inc.

KEYS TO SUCCESS:

- Build a company around a focus on quality and manufacturing excellence.
- Nurture your relationships with your sales force or dealer network. In the final analysis, the customer really experiences your product through them.
- Stand behind your product with an exceptional guarantee, and customers will pay a premium price.
- Have a succession plan.
- Realize that tough times can be an opportunity to gain market share.
- Know that there is a lot to be said for being a private family business. You can do things without second-guessing.
- Understand the risks you're willing to take, and make sure your financial plan is consistent with that strategy.
- A family needs to be visible and decisive in times of crisis to let employees and vendors know that the business will come back.

Contact information for Jayco, Inc.:

> Jayco, Inc.
> 903 South Main St.
> P.O. Box 460
> Middlebury, IN 46540
> Phone: 574-825-5861
> Wilbur L. Bontrager, Chief Executive Officer
> E-mail: Wilbur_bontrager@jayco.com
> *www.jayco.com*

4) Six-year-old Entrepreneur Implements His Business Plan

Wes Culver Realty

This six-year-old had a plan, and he started implementing it right away. First he identified a market when he noticed workers on his family duck farm were always thirsty, so he made a deal to buy cases of soda from the local Pepsi driver for a nickel a can. He put the cans in the refrigerator where they kept the worms for the bait shop and sold them via self-service to the farm workers and customers at the bait shop for ten cents. Pretty soon he was selling four or five cases a week and rolling in dough. He also had his first failure when he tried to sell Hi-C to the same group. The problem was that his mom served Hi-C in the house, so it wasn't a treat. Nobody bought it.

Not to be dismayed, Wes Culver told his brothers he had a plan. When he grew up, he wanted to own one hundred businesses, each earning a dollar a month. He could already see the power of diversification, vertical integration, and multiple revenue streams.

Throughout his formative years he had many small businesses and side jobs. When he went to the local, conservative Mennonite Goshen College, he convinced them to let him have a phone in his room, because by then he had his own small duck farm and was doing buying and selling all the time while clearing $50,000 a year on a part-time job.

His plan took a little sidetrack when he married Val and decided to devote himself to Christ. He became an associate pastor, making $6,800 per year. He loved the work and ran several Bible study groups, getting to know many people in the local area and developing solid relationships with them. When Val and Wes started having kids, Val couldn't keep her part-time jobs and take care of the kids. Plus, she was no longer interested in getting up at 3:00 AM on Sundays to help in Wes's latest scheme, a goose farm, where he was selling goose eggs each week. Wes sold the goose farm and got his Realtor's license on a lark.

Now what was he to do? Well, he knew a bunch of people, so he started calling them. He set a goal to call at least ten people per week. He asked them all if they knew of someone who might be buying or selling a house. Since he had a huge network and was respected for his work ethic and integrity, he quickly got a herd of people following him. Within a couple years, he was the number one selling Realtor in Elkhart County, and he started his own brokerage firm.

Let's just say he's exceeded the business plan he sketched out in his head when he was six years old. He might not own one hundred businesses right now (he's not sure how many he actually owns, but hopes his bookkeeper does). Chances are that with all the businesses he's owned, founded, joint ventured, financed, etc., he's probably well over one hundred. And he has been a very successful businessman.

All the while, he's maintained a quiet, unassuming demeanor and devotion to his family and God. He's been a pastor a few more times in his career and is still heavily involved with his Church and local charities. When you meet him and talk to him, there is no hint of the swagger he really should be able to demonstrate, because almost everything he gets involved with is successful. Sure, he's had his failures, but Wes's failures are like most of us when we succeed. He says the only business that has consistently generated a loss is the bed and breakfast he owns on some of his family's land. Even that has turned around in the last year or two and is now in positive cash flow.

So what's Wes's business? Well, as best we could tell when we got together, here's the list:

- Six real estate offices in Northern Indiana and Southern Michigan under the umbrella of Wes Culver/Prudential One Realty
- A property management company that includes landscaping services
- A home and small office construction company
- A remodeling and handyman business
- A bed and breakfast
- An alarm company that installs home and office security systems
- A dump trailer company (Work Easy Trailers, which manufactures small trailers)
- Prudential Properties, which owns several of his realty buildings and some other properties
- Numerous other real estate partnerships which own buildings and land, along with some doing real estate development
- A used car business (of which he is a part owner; he is very hands-off and is not sure where it is located right now)
- Two real estate broker licensing schools

He's also owned title companies, mortgage companies, and an insurance agency. Oh, by the way, he just bought Work Easy Trailers in October of 2008, right when the financial markets were melting down and he was in the middle of his campaign for Indiana state representative (see below). He always wanted to own a manufacturing company. It seemed like a more stable business to him, since you can just set up processes and do the same thing every day. And he just sold the heating and air-conditioning company that he had owned for about a year. One of the partners wanted to run it on his own, so Wes said, "Fine," and sold his interest.

And as another thing, he and some partners have now started a gourmet exotic jerky business, selling exclusively on the Internet. It's called *PaulsJerky.com,* and it carries alligator, duck, ostrich, kangaroo, and buffalo jerky. It's just getting off the ground, and he's looking for suppliers.

Finally, Wes tells me he has an idea for a themed clothing business. It's so good, he won't tell me what the theme is, but he's sure it will be a multi-million-dollar business.

When pressed about the reasons for the various businesses, he said many came from a philosophy that he always wants to be his own best customer. Therefore, many current and former businesses revolve around the real estate business. He also tells people to let him know about good opportunities, so they come his way all the time. If the business isn't directly related to the real estate business, he tries to see what the issues are and whether he can have an impact. Some just don't have the capital to be successful, and others aren't able to market effectively. Others need management. I get the impression that Wes deals only with people he trusts, and if he spots a problem, he makes a quick change. And he's happy to be an opportunist and take advantage of a bargain when he sees one. In short, there is no one formula, just a lot of judgment and willingness to accept risk.

Wes considers himself an idea man who's easily bored by the day-to-day operations of the businesses. Doing deals and spotting new opportunities are his passions. He really delegates well. He has a few key people he relies on—a very lean staff. He makes sure his bookkeeper is on top of the numbers, and he watches them like a hawk. He knows how each business is doing, what sales trends are, and what his costs and margins are looking like.

Personal tragedy struck Wes, Val, and their family in 2002 when their oldest son, Chad, was killed in a horrible motorcycle accident in his freshman year at Indiana University. Wes admits he lost some zest for life at that point, and he wondered about whether he should continue all his business ventures. He questioned why he was building his mini empire, since he always considered a primary reason for doing all this was to pass the business on to the next generation of his family. Faith in God, personal resilience, and the support of his friends and business associates got him through it all.

Testament to Wes and Val's faith was evident when they adopted a Chinese baby girl, Cydney, just a few years after Chad's death. I don't know of many people who could respond in such a fashion. Wes and Val have two other children; Craig, an Indiana University graduate who sells real estate for Wes, and Chelsea, a student at Ball State University.

Now back to the Indiana state representative thing—Wes is conservative politically, socially, and fiscally. He says that like most of us, he complained often about the things he saw happening with our government. But he also has had the plan to run for political office for many years. He wanted to make sure he was secure financially and also that his family was on firm footing. He made comments to a few friends that he'd like to run for office some day but never really pursued it. In the summer of 2007, he decided he was ready and prayed to God to open the door for him, if that was the plan.

That winter, while on vacation in Florida, he got a call from someone in his home district asking if he'd ever considered running for State Representative. Wes said yes, but he knew that there was a strong incumbent in his district. What he found was that there was a quiet undercurrent to unseat the incumbent. Wes was asked to attend a meeting in Elkhart. He flew home, and after a few minutes with some local leaders, he decided to run—but they told him they could not support him financially until after the primary. They told him they couldn't afford to antagonize the incumbent if Wes didn't beat him. And they told him he would need at least $100,000 to win the office.

Wes went to Indianapolis and garnered some political and financial support from various business leaders—so he was literally off to the political races. And he dove in like it was the last race of his life. During the primary and November elections he raised more than $120,000 and put in $20,000 of his own money. As party leaders started to see his tenacity and learned about his conservative values, they started to come on board. Campaign veterans showed up to advise and help. He won both the primary and November elections in a landslide. Of course, there were cries of "foul" from some of the opposition as their futile attempts to meet Wes's challenge were thwarted.

Even more so than the other executives interviewed for this book, Wes is actually putting his views out there for all of us to examine by holding public office. He is staunchly anti-tax and has already rallied his fellow representatives to support legislation that gives taxpayers a break. Wes's view is that those in Elkhart County are speaking out of both sides of our mouths when they talk about fiscal conservatism, yet ask for federal and state bailout money. Wes's philosophy is simple: reduce taxes and keep government out of our lives. He thinks we all have a personal responsibility to know the issues and back a good candidate who supports our values. If you think that candidate isn't running for office, help to draft someone who will represent you right—or run yourself.

As a freshman state representative, Wes hasn't been bashful about expressing himself. He loves what he's doing and feels he is having an impact already. His focus is on doing his job for the people he represents, but he knows that a two-year term isn't enough time to make the meaningful change he believes is necessary. He's already putting together his plan for re-election. When pressed about further political plans, Wes was coy, but you get the impression he won't be content for long. With his intelligence, executive abilities, and strong family values, he could be a leader for years to come—and at higher levels.

With the current economic situation, Wes's main strategy is to go where the money is. His property management company is growing, so he's opening a new office in South Bend. Construction is a long way off, but real estate sales are okay. He is aggressively trying to grow his alarm company and the new dump trailer company. He's trying to restructure his finances and believes his best bet is to hold on to his many properties until values come back. However, the climate for dealing with banks is tough, since they have become so risk averse. But he always has a philosophy of dealing with multiple banks so he has options. He estimates he has more than ten banks which have loans with him right now.

Wes says he's ready to try something completely different in his business career. Some plans are in place to take him even further from the daily oversight of his real estate business. As mentioned earlier, he has some other ideas for Internet businesses. He says there has never been a master plan for his career, so he really has no idea what the next moves might be.

Wes Culver is the kind of man who makes you wonder how he does it all and makes it look so easy. He's successful at his businesses and stays on top of them. He has a wonderful family and is active in his church. He also has hobbies including riding motorcycles and running several miles a week. And despite all of this, he's a politician who has taken a $20,000-a-year job and sacrifices time away from his family. Our country has made it very difficult for people like Wes to run for office. We ask them to give up so much and criticize everything they do. If only we had more people like Wes Culver who would stand up for us, I believe we'd be in a much better place.

Wes Culver Realty
KEYS TO SUCCESS:

- Dream big.
- Don't be afraid to take a risk, even a business is one you aren't totally familiar with.
- Rely on your faith in God to get you through tough times and show you the plan.
- Keep family first.
- Look for opportunities to be your own best customer.
- Diversify and nurture multiple sources of income.
- Build your network and work your network.
- In tough times, go where the money is.
- Spread your financial exposure by using multiple banks.
- Use your talents to serve your community, your state, and your country.
- Be immune to criticism.
- Constantly reinvent yourself and your company.

Contact information if you want to know more about Wes Culver Home Team/Prudential One Realty or contact Wes:

Prudential One Realty
Attention: Wes Culver
2020-B Elkhart Road
Goshen, IN 46526
Phone: 574-534-HOME
Business Web site: *www.wesculver.com*
State Representative Web site: *www.in.gov/h49*
E-mail: wesculver@wesculver.com

5) Somebody Forgot the Silver Spoon

Troyer Foods

Paris and Becky Ball-Miller are successful entrepreneurs and the sole owners of a company with more than $235 million in sales, operating in five states and with 280 employees. They play golf together at the local country club and take nice vacations. They own an airplane to travel between distribution centers and have just completed pilot training to earn their instrument ratings. Some newer employees and community members assume this charmed existence is just that—the product of a silver spoon in their mouths. But the reality is much, much different.

Paris's parents divorced when he was eight years old and his father was incarcerated in Texas for spousal abuse. His mother had multiple health problems and was disabled most of the time until she died when Paris was fourteen. Paris lived with extreme poverty and can remember times when his mother sent him to the neighbors to beg for food. He spent much time in foster homes and orphanages growing up, finally spending his high school time living with relatives in Indiana. He was a poor student in high school because he had no direction or hope for his future. His plan was to enter the military after high school, and he had enlisted, but at the last minute changed his mind because the military life reminded him of horrible memories of living in an orphanage. Through the grace of God and some generous benefactors, he was given the opportunity to attend Manchester

College in northern Indiana, which he did only because there were no better options.

At Manchester, he started to realize he was just as smart as other people, and if he worked hard he could get good grades. He chose an accounting major only because the college had a good reputation in accounting, and he observed that the accounting grads generally got jobs. He also met Becky at Manchester. He graduated in 1981.

During the next few years, Paris had good jobs at Big Eight CPA firms and as a controller at one or two other companies. In 1988, he noticed a newspaper ad for a seemingly small food company in Goshen, Indiana and applied. He was hired as the chief financial officer at Troyer Foods.

Troyer Foods was a family business started in 1948 by Elroy and Al Troyer on a farm in Vandalia, Michigan. They raised and sold chickens primarily to restaurants. The business was small enough that Al left after a few years, but other family members joined during the '50s and '60s, and the company steadily grew, expanding from just poultry distribution to a full line of food products. In 1964, they moved into the present facility just outside of Goshen. A new generation of Troyers came into the business, but Elroy was still hanging on. The family thought the only way to get him to retire was to sell the business, which was accomplished for a tidy sum in early 1988. Paris was brought in to replace Elroy's brother, Ora, who handled finances, and he was to work side by side with Elroy's sons. Paris was the first non-Troyer to hold a decision-making position in Troyer's history, and it was a very challenging period. At the time, the company had about $175 million in sales and 180 employees with full-line foodservice distribution to restaurants and grocery stores.

The next several years were tumultuous. The sons all had three-year contracts and left around 1991. At this point, Paris was named general manager of the operation, a hard pill to swallow for some because he wasn't a Troyer. The purchasers of the business were from England, and they had many internal problems, as well as squabbles with their U. S. and Canadian subsidiaries. And the Troyer operation was never able to achieve the same level of profits the family had accomplished. So the company was put up for sale two or three times, but because they had overpaid for the business initially, the new owners couldn't bring themselves to sell at a reasonable price.

Finally the situation came to a boil in the 1995–1996 timeframe when the parent company fell on very tough times and was forced to liquidate many assets. The Canadian subsidiary was quickly sold, but there were still no takers for Troyer's. Paris's boss suggested that Paris consider buying the company, which he had not previously seriously considered because of all the turmoil, the continuing strain with the Troyers, and a very tough corporate culture. Paris was prepared to move on to the next phase in his career once a buyer was secured.

But he went home to Becky and told her he wanted to buy the company. By this time, Becky had established herself in her career as executive director of Camp Mack, a Christian retreat center. Becky is a PK ("Preacher's Kid") and is herself an ordained minister in the Church of the Brethren. Her full-time job was running this 200-acre camp, and she had been quite successful. Paris and Becky actually lived on the grounds of the camp as part of her compensation plan. Becky was happy with their lives and felt they had good financial stability. In fact, over the years, Paris and Becky had followed a very conservative family financial strategy. They have no kids and had decided they would always try to live off the least of their salaries (which at the time was Becky's $8,200 per year). Her father had taught her this strategy to never have to rely on someone else, and Paris embraced it because of the poverty in his early life. So they had a nice nest egg saved up, which Paris now wanted to use as equity for the purchase of Troyer's.

The first idea for the potential purchase came in June of 1996. The next several months were a roller coaster. After some initial concerns, Becky was fully behind the deal. Both Paris and Becky were working their business contacts for potential bank financing. Paris was talking to some bigger banks, which never came through after months of talking, many proposals, and finally, no real commitment letters. The deal was eventually financed through a small local bank which had done business with Becky at Camp Mack.

During the ensuing months, Paris got wind that one of the Troyer sons who had been out of the business for five years was trying to buy the company back. Paris assumed he was being used to get the price up for the sellers. After the fact, he found out that one of the investors in the son's group was their biggest customer, a local chain of supermarkets. (They lost this customer after the purchase, but got them back about three years later.) Because of all the uncertainty and turmoil, five of the main product buyers in the company walked out right before Thanksgiving, one of the biggest sales weeks of the year in the food business. In late 1996 the deal was finalized.

Becky was still at her job, but Paris immersed himself in Troyer's. New people were hired for those who had left. He changed the compensation system for drivers to a pay-for-performance model he had copied from a competitor and faced a potential unionization. As mentioned, they lost their biggest customer, and sales declined to $135 million. But through it all, the company remained profitable. They were highly leveraged, having completed the acquisition for $9 million, a combination of their life savings and bank debt. So the margin for error was thin, and their mentality was to just survive three years. They also implemented a new profit-sharing plan for all employees, which started paying out right away. This helped to build teamwork and morale.

Guess who is now the CEO of Troyer Foods? Would you believe it's the ordained minister and former camp director, Becky? How she got there is a story in itself.

Paris was having great success. He had survived the first few years and now had his feet underneath him. Things were becoming more manageable, and he knew he could do this. Becky was also thriving and had completed a major anniversary celebration at Camp Mack in 2000; plus she had made plans for a major expansion and construction project. On a brief sabbatical in the summer of 2001, she started to notice that things didn't feel right. She had been at Camp Mack twenty-four years and had no intention of leaving, but she asked God if that was really his plan for her. The answer became apparent to her that it was time to leave. So she told the board and announced she would resign effective January 1, 2002, with a fully planned transition.

The first few months after the resignation date were filled with tying up loose ends at Camp Mack and commitments she had to some other ministries and as president of the national Christian camp trade association. In March, Paris came home and made a strange request. The Troyer's sales department was having morale and effectiveness problems, so he needed some help. Would Becky be willing to come on in an interim role as sales director? She thought about it and met with the rest of the management team to make sure they were okay with this. She came on right before the annual food show.

The next year Becky became an integral part of the company. Her skills in management and organizational development were evident. Plus her background as a minister and her charismatic personality drew many employees to her. By the end of the first year, Troyer decided to hire another sales director and make Becky executive vice president.

In the last few years, Troyer Foods has made three acquisitions, including two smaller food service distributors and a meat cutting operation in southern Indiana. As they embarked on these acquisitions, they found that it could be advantageous to be a Woman Business Enterprise (WBE). There is an organization that certifies WBEs, and this can result in access to various government loan programs and/or vendor preference in some bidding processes. So Paris took the step of formally transferring ownership of 51 percent to Becky and named her chief executive officer. Paris is president.

In fact, the company is run by the two as partners, much as a mother and father function in a family. While Paris focuses on systems and may be a little more analytical ("realistic," as he says), Becky is the cheerleader and is very comfortable being the voice to the public. Paris has less patience for whining and every once in a while has to tell someone his story if they think a driver's salary of $50,000 is tough to survive on.

The company's mantra has become "A Company of Destination." They take their commitment to quality and service very seriously and believe this will draw their customers to them. Similarly, Becky has especially brought the view that you serve through your people, so they have to treat each other with respect, have a team atmosphere, pay well, and in short, be a place where people want to work. (Paris cites that turnover has declined from around 100 percent before the purchase by Becky and Paris to less than 10 percent last year.) Finally, they are quite serious about creating vendor relationships that are win-win.

They believe they have created a new way of doing business—a new corporate culture. This new culture has been blended and adapted as the acquisitions have been assimilated.

The company is very involved in the community, with numerous charities they give to or are active in. Paris is on the local hospital board of directors, and Becky is on the local mental health hospital board and the Economic Development Corporation. Out of date or damaged food is given to several food banks. Employees are also encouraged to be active, with many corporate teams sponsored for walks, runs, etc.

We only had a few minutes to discuss the current situation in Elkhart County, but Paris remains concerned about the area's reliance on the RV industry. Health care is a major issue, because they try to provide adequate health insurance for their employees, but it's a major challenge with escalating costs. Becky is optimistic that our economy will come back and believes in the goodwill which exists in the hearts of most of us. So she thinks the county will work through its problems and thrive again.

Troyer's is a staple business built on service, people, systems, and relationships. As long as the county has restaurants and grocery stores, it will need these products and services. It's a competitive business, with multiple national and regional companies vying for the same space. Paris and Becky have built upon the original family legacy with a tough resilience gained by knowing where they came from and how hard they worked to make it. And they have been able to combine a service mentality and love of people to build a team poised to grow and become a premier Midwest foodservice organization.

<u>Troyer Foods</u>

KEYS TO SUCCESS:

- The American Dream is really alive; you can do whatever you want to do, even if you have never heard of a silver spoon.
- Don't be afraid to change your role or apply your skills in different ways—an accountant with almost no money can buy a company, and a camp director can become a CEO.
- Treat people well, and they will serve your customers the same way.
- A good team can accomplish even more, so look for growth opportunities in times when everyone else is throwing in the towel.

Contact information:

Troyer's Foods
P.O. Box 608
Goshen, IN 46527
Phone: 574-533-0302
Toll-free: 800-876-9377
www.troyers.com
Becky Ball-Miller, CEO
E-mail: becky@troyers.com
Paris Ball-Miller, President
E-mail: paris@troyers.com

6) Your Money Is Safe in This Bank

First State Bank of Middlebury

"Your Money Is Safe in This Bank" was the headline from an advertisement in the local Middlebury, Indiana newspaper on November 8, 1918 after the First State Bank of Middlebury had thwarted an armed robbery attempt because the safe was so strong and foolproof that the robbers gave up trying to get in. The bank took advantage of the publicity from the situation and reminded the community of what a safe place the bank was for their money, stressing how it was also impervious to fire. Another time, an armed robbery was halted when tellers triggered an alarm system connected to the police station and some other businesses in town, resulting in some of the businesspeople coming with their shotguns, which had been stored under their desks.

Conservative and *safe* are two adjectives that First State Bank has lived by for its ninety-nine years and which have served them well. The bank uses the tagline "Hometown Values," and its annual report shows a picture of the bank with a street sign saying, "We are Main Street." Perhaps you are starting to get the idea that this isn't one of the banks that led us down the primrose path to the housing crisis.

Jim Hiatt, the president of First State Bank of Middlebury since 1982, is representative of the typical board member for the bank, a board that is active and remains true to its hometown roots.

Most members are businesspeople in the local community. At times, Jim has wanted to move quicker than they have, but they have always worked it out, because there is mutual respect and an understanding of the overall goal, which is to remain independent and have the strength to provide the right level of service for small businesses and families in Middlebury and surrounding regions.

Jim arrived at the bank in 1982 right at the end of the Jimmy Carter recession, when they were still dealing with 20 percent interest rates and high inflation. In Jim's opinion, the RV and manufactured housing industry was even worse off then than what we are seeing now. Because of Jim's tenure in his job and his standing in the Indiana banking community, he was able to offer a unique perspective on the current crisis and how the county got there. He's also the board chair for the Elkhart Development Corporation (EDC), which is the county's primary recruiter of new businesses to the area.

Jim has observed the relative boom of the years since 1982. Blessed with a strong local workforce, much of which is Amish, the industry saw continued growth. Entrepreneurs were starting new companies to either make the RVs or supply parts to the factories. Some of the companies sold out to larger national or international companies. Jim thinks this management from afar contributed to a go-go mentality, resulting in overcapacity. With the excess capacity, cutthroat competition started to raise its ugly head. Low margins became an issue. The area's biggest strength became a real curse when the sales started to flatten and even decline a few years ago. Then Hurricane Katrina hit, and there was a huge need for the area's RVs and small modular homes. This demand masked the industry's problems for a year or two—problems which many insiders knew would soon haunt them.

The Elkhart area became an anomaly in the country with a rising number of manufacturing jobs which paid very well, especially due to an incentive-based payment system. Many workers made

$50,000 to $75,000 for semi-skilled jobs. At one point, Jim said that Middlebury was known as the town with a population of 1,000 with daily manufacturing jobs of 5,000. Coachmen and Jayco are two of the best-known industry names headquartered in Middlebury. Jayco is still family owned (see Chapter 3), but Coachmen is a public company, and in 2008 they actually sold their core RV business. Now they focus on making buses.

After the Katrina blip, interest rates started to rise, and gasoline prices became a major issue. All of sudden, demand dried up as the country started to sort out the banking crisis and bursting housing bubble. Lenders exacerbated the problem as they pulled their dealer and consumer financing for RVs. Jim attributes some of this to the fact that many of the banks—like the RV companies—now have absentee owners who don't have as much invested financially and emotionally as those who have lived and grown up in the community.

Jim's observations about the local leaders is that many thought the RV boom would never end and therefore weren't interested in attracting new business. Some had even asserted that they would never give incentives to new businesses, and now these same leaders are jumping on the bandwagon to partner with the EDC to lure new companies with many promises and incentives. The same leaders are also doing everything they can to attract federal stimulus money and also get the State of Indiana to help.

Jim, his board members, and other bank executives remain active and visible in development efforts, economic planning, and community issues, because First State Bank and the communities are inextricably linked. Before the Great Depression, as many as twelve community banks operated in Elkhart County. FSB of Middlebury is the lone survivor today. Eighteen different bank franchises now operate in Elkhart County, as well as several credit unions. Obviously, Jim thinks this field is way too crowded, but he's not whining about it. His bank continues to grow, and every few years a new branch is opened. The bank now has branches in Goshen, Elkhart, and Mishawaka. The Mishawaka branch is in a growing retail and office park area and represents the first foray into another county (St. Joseph County, where South Bend and Notre Dame are located). When its headquarters are in a town of 3,500, these new markets represent huge potential growth for First State Bank.

As banks have grown and evolved over the years, we have seen a tremendous consolidation. Mergers and acquisitions have happened at a fever pitch for twenty to thirty years. In somewhat of a backlash, small community banks have sprung up. Many have succeeded to a point, but many others have also been gobbled up, which is disappointing to some. Through it all, First State Bank has remained totally independent. One of the key reasons is that they have never had any one party own more than 10 percent of the bank's stock. The board has taken pride in its independence, and although some would make a nice sum if the bank were sold, they've been true to this core philosophy.

During Jim's tenure, the assets of the bank have risen from $30 million to more than $400 million. If the truth were to be told, my reading is that they'd still be closer to $30 million if they could have seen a way to do it. But Jim was scanning the market and making assessments of what would be necessary to continue to meet their mission. And he became convinced that being so small would not allow the necessary investments in new services and technology the industry and its customers were becoming used to.

Here are just a few of the innovations that have allowed the bank to grow:

- During the 1970s, the bank had one of the state's first drive-thru tellers.
- They also had the first drive-thru ATM in Elkhart County.
- They have embraced online banking and now offer a special product, 21st Century Checking, which features

online banking, loan incentives, and free checking. The idea is to promote electronic banking, because it saves the bank and the customer money.

- The main office and its branches are connected by microwave satellite technology, which is relatively sophisticated and high speed. This allows for secure transmission of data and other features such as video conferencing for management and staff meetings.
- The new Mishawaka branch is totally cashless—again the first of its kind in the state of Indiana. So for the bank, which seems like the one place where your five-year-old could bring his pennies for his savings account, they've gone completely the other way. The emphasis at that branch is small businesses and wealthy individuals, so the branch is staffed with well-trained customer service people who can respond to the specific needs of these niche customers. The branch opened without a lot of fanfare a few years ago and has grown rapidly.

As mentioned, a conservative lending philosophy has kept First State Bank stable even in these tough times. They have always tried to have a very personal relationship with their customers, knowing most by name. Jim says they look for businesses which are led by people with integrity, because in tough times, you can count on these people to live up to their promises. It's a two-way street, so in these times, Jim and the loan officers are doing everything they can to be proactive—to restructure loans or help the loan customers find alternatives that will help their situation. They've even done some matchmaking by connecting customers who might be able to do business with each other.

Here's a story that won't be told in many boardrooms across this nation. Keep in mind that First State Bank sits in the heart of an Amish community. Many of the Amish have small farms and businesses. Others work in the RV industry. So they have been hit by the economic downturn also. They have ways to track the national and local news, but virtually none use the Internet, watch TV, etc. Communicating with them can be tough, and Jim was concerned that they may not know how to react if their home mortgages or business loans got behind.

The Amish organize themselves in small church areas run by bishops. One bishop may have twenty or thirty families he leads, and this area can cover just a few square miles. First State Bank got the word out to the bishops that they were having a special meeting to discuss the economic situation. The Bank invited them into a weeknight dinner meeting and had a frank discussion about what was happening, how the Amish were being affected, and how to respond. The message was that the bank didn't want them to just give up or feel ashamed if they missed some loan payments. Jim urged the bishops to tell their people who were having trouble to come into the bank and talk with them about alternatives. Jim and the Bank know the Amish can be counted on and that they are good customers, so he wants to make sure they help each other through this mess. What a refreshing change from the horror stories about people being foreclosed by institutions who just see them as a number or by the organizations who bought the subprime loans and are just liquidating their investments.

As Jim and I talked about the political situation, he is horrified by leadership at the top of our country, including leadership over the last several years. He recanted the poor decision-making by Alan Greenspan and the congressional oversight of people like Barney Frank and Chris Dodd, who now sit in judgment of the organizations like Fannie Mae and Freddie Mac, when they were previously proponents. He mentioned the poor oversight by the SEC and the lack of leadership by the Bush administration leading to the massive bailouts in the fall of 2008. And he is convinced that the Obama administration's huge stimulus plan will put us in very dire economic straits.

Leadership at the Indiana state level has been very good with Governor Mitch Daniels. The decision to lease the Indiana Toll Road has provided a major source of capital to the state which will pay off for years to come and relieve us of the Toll Road's tax and management burden. Jim also knows that we need to be preparing the next generation of workers, who need to be much more skilled than the typical RV worker. So he's been pushing for community and state college branches in Elkhart County. While the county has had some success, some political leaders in neighboring Democratic counties are reluctant to work with this largely Republican county. Jim sees this as cutting off its nose to spite its face, because regional economic planning is a key to attracting new business and maximizing the area's potential.

Another thread running through the bank, its staff, and its leadership is a strong sense of patriotism. As you walk through the bank, you see many images of the American flag and remembrances of soldiers who have served our country. I've played in several golf outings where First State Bank players can be recognized by the flags on their golf carts, and you always find a golf towel with the American flag on it. Several current and retired officers and staff of the bank are leaders in the local American Legion and can be seen fixing the flags which drape downtown Middlebury, marching in the summer parade, and organizing the all-night vigil in the Middlebury cemetery over Memorial Day weekend to honor our local veterans who have died. I'm convinced this patriotism is one of the key values which may not be in their business plan, but which is part of the culture of the bank and which has a dramatic influence on how they do business.

As we talked about how First State Bank is faring right now, Jim is thankful for their conservative philosophy. The bank hasn't really had any major cutbacks and is still growth oriented. Income is down some, but liquidity is good, and the bank is still lending much as it always had. The primary reasons for income being down are the increased loan loss reserves to reflect the finances of many of their customers who are hurting right now. Jim also mentioned that increased assessments from governmental organizations like FDIC have risen dramatically and will be up more than ten times to more than $1 million for the current fiscal year. The Bank chose not to take Troubled Asset Relief Program (TARP) funds and is now very glad they didn't, given the problems experienced by banks who took TARP funds. The intrusion into decision-making by the government definitely goes against the independent grain of First State Bank, so Jim is relieved they made this decision.

As First State Bank looks to the next decade, Jim is convinced they will still be a major player in the Elkhart market—but don't look for any radical shift in strategy and major growth. Stressing solid personal relationships has always been a strength, and every new strategy will be evaluated against this hometown approach. They may open their stock ownership to the public markets more than in the past to provide additional capital. A few more branches will probably be opened up, and Jim doesn't eliminate the possibility of buying another small, regional bank with a similar customer base which may not have been as successful financially.

As long as the government policies allow for small banks like this to operate independently, Jim sees First State Bank being essentially the same as it has been for the last hundred years or so. A safe oasis in the desert of troubled financial institutions, a place hometown customers can count on, and an organization that helps the local community by working side by side with its members—that's what Jim and First State Bank want to be for the next hundred years.

First State Bank of Middlebury

KEYS TO SUCCESS:

- Focus on your core community—it's your base.
- Build your business to serve your core community.
- Control your destiny by remaining independent.
- Build a personal relationship with each customer so that when times are tough you can trust each other.
- Be careful in the implementation of new technology, but make sure you don't get too far behind the technology curve. Even small businesses can be leaders in some technological strategies.
- Truly embrace your community, and work with them. Provide leadership, and choose ways to help financially. Sit at the table to craft the future.
- Realize basic economics always come back to haunt you, so don't stretch too far to make a deal. Be a rock that your customers can rely on.
- Know that safe, steady hometown values built our country. Be proud of your country, and don't be afraid to proclaim your patriotism.

Contact information for First State Bank of Middlebury:

First State Bank of Middlebury
111 S. Main Street
P.O. Box 69
Middlebury, IN 46540
www.fsbmiddlebury.com
James G. Hiatt, President and CEO
E-mail: jghiatt@fsbmiddlebury.com

7) Build It and They Will Come (or Vice Versa?)

Language Art

This is the story of an almost accidental business—but not really. You see, this business was envisioned and perhaps developed providentially, and its owners, Greg and Dilynn Puckett, seized opportunity when it appeared and have not looked back. Every step hasn't been easy, and they still don't have a business plan, but they continue growing at a rapid pace, generating great cash flow and a very comfortable income for the artistic couple.

The business is called Language Art, and to really get a feel for what they do, I'd recommend going to their Web site right now, *www.languageartonline.com*. I've actually known Greg and Dilynn casually from our local community for a few years. I had shopped in the quaint antique shop that they had for just a few years. My wife bought some of Dilynn's custom beaded polymer jewelry at some local festivals, but we had no idea they had entered this new venture, especially with such success. They have essentially created a new product category which has been a star in the slumping gift shop retail industry.

What they do is create uplifting and inspirational word signs using photos of scenes from architecture, nature, and old signs which resemble the letters of the alphabet. My wife had purchased a sign for our sister-in-law with the word "BELIEVE" on it, and the gift was a huge hit. Later, when someone told us about the Pucketts' new business, we realized it was their product. They have several stock phrases and signs you can buy. Each letter is a black and white image which is mounted on a four-by-six-inch piece of wood with clear glass covering the photo. The letters are assembled together to create the sign.

Greg is a process engineer by training and worked in traditional engineering jobs until 1998. At that time, he ventured out on his own, doing some freelance engineering consulting. He also helped Dilynn with the jewelry business and the antique store. They always dreamed of finding a business where they could work side by side and had prayed for such an opportunity.

Dilynn is quite artistic and is an accomplished photographer. (Greg also studied photography in college.) The two saw photography as a great hobby to share and used every trip or special occasion as a photographic opportunity. For a few years, Dilynn actually kept a photo journal, taking a daily picture to remember what happened and what struck her about life, family, the community, etc. She also noticed that some of the photos looked like letters and started to take more letter pictures just for fun.

When she was showing some friends her photography they commented on the photo letters and said that there ought to be a way to make them into some signs. Greg and Dilynn went to work and made fifteen signs, which they put out along with Dilynn's jewelry at the Middlebury Fall Festival in the fall of 2006. The signs sold immediately.

Now they thought they had something, and luckily a local upscale gift shop owner with two shops saw the product and asked to have it in her stores. So Greg and Dilynn started regular production and supplied these two shops. Gradually this grew to about ten shops. The product was noticed by an industry trade journal, *Gift Beat,* and they got a favorable article written. It was suggested that they set up a booth at a Chicago Retail Gift show. They knew this could be the impetus to a real business, so they had to think long and hard about this.

Both had kept active in other jobs and business ventures which were paying the bills, but this could take them in a direction they had always dreamed about. As Greg says, "We prayed about the opportunity to work together and whether this was the right business for us. We decided if the Lord took us in this direction, we would follow his lead."

So they signed up for the show in July of 2007. The first day they had three people working the booth and were swamped all day long taking orders. At the end of the day, there was an exhibitor meeting, and everyone was singing the blues about how slow the show was and the lack of orders. Greg and Dilynn were tired and pleased, but they didn't know whether they were doing well or not.

Going into the show, they had hoped for ten new customers. After the show, they had 150 new retail stores who agreed to carry the product! And they won the show's top prize for Retailers' Choice Award. On the trip back to Middlebury, Dilynn broke into tears and said, "Can't we just tell them we were kidding?"

Up until now they had continued to assemble the signs in the living room. Now they had to find production space and an office—plus they needed to streamline their production process, source materials, and hire production people just to fill the orders from the show. They had taken orders for product they really had no idea how to fulfill. Their faith in their product, their abilities, and God got them through this.

Greg says the fall of 2007 was very tough, but exciting. They had several slip-ups with suppliers and couldn't get product out the door quickly enough, so they had to delay shipments several times. By staying in constant communication with the retailers,

Greg thinks this whole situation actually worked to their benefit as the idea of scarcity made the product seem more unique and valuable, creating even more pent-up demand.

Over the past few years they have attended more trade shows, including the biggest international show in Atlanta. Their product is carried by more than 550 stores in 40 states, Aruba, and Canada. The product can be purchased off their Web site, but they haven't promoted that much as they want to have the retail stores feel that the Web site isn't competing with them. The retail stores receive exclusivity within their ZIP code, as long as they meet minimum volumes.

From a financial perspective, Greg and Dilynn require every customer to pay in advance with a credit card, thus drastically reducing their risk and avoiding the need to track accounts receivable. This keeps the finances simple and improves cash flow. A few times they have been pushed on this issue, even by a chain of more than 150 stores. Greg has maintained this policy and never really lost any business because of it.

Sales have risen steadily. In their first full year of operation the company achieved around $750,000 in sales, and only about $30,000 of that was online. Greg and Dilynn are really the only two managers at the company, and they have approximately ten part-time, stay-at-home moms who work in the assembly and shipping area. At first they produced five days a week (generally production hours are 9:00 AM to 3:00 PM to accommodate the moms' schedules). Now they can produce more in three days per week with efficiency. Sales for 2009 should approach $1 million.

Greg and Dilynn have good instincts and complementary skills. While they have some goals for the business, it appears they don't want to stray too far from what they have done so far. They have dabbled with a line of note cards with their photo art and have a new line called "Language Art Expressions," which are smaller letters that are purchased as a set and can be put in a tray to make the customer's own message as the mood strikes them. The business has been designed to fit their family and marriage goals first, so they don't want to allow it to control them. Greg hopes for steady continued growth—possibly to around the $10 million mark.

There really is no business plan other that what the two partners may discuss over lunch or dinner. Greg says he has done a lot of formal planning in prior careers, and so far he has been able to manage the two-plus years without extensive plans. Income for the partners has well exceeded what either has made in the past.

The marketing approach has been similarly Spartan. There are few sales pieces, catalogues, or brochures. Potential customers are shown the product at shows and told to go to the website, which has a special area for wholesale customers. Greg and Dilynn do little in formal communication or direct mail to customers, but Greg does use monthly e-mails to let them know what's happening. With the relatively small number of customers, Greg and Dilynn pretty much know each by name and talk with them by phone regularly.

Three or four copycat competitors have crept up. The language art idea is not patentable, but they have copyrighted their photos. Greg pays little attention to the competitors but hears about them from some customers. Artistically, Greg and Dilynn are pleased with their own product, and their customers have been happy with their products and service. So Greg sees no need to study the competition, which might make them consciously or subconsciously respond in a fashion that alters their successful formula.

Greg and Dilynn are religiously conservative and not too involved politically. They've grown up in the area and know many in the RV industry well. To that extent, they are very concerned about where the industry is headed. Greg wonders whether the upcoming generation may not be into camping and the RV lifestyle like the fifty-plus crowd. He's also a proponent of getting more diversified businesses in the area so that there are more jobs and opportunities for young people. But he thinks the media has really oversold the misery in Elkhart County. His observation is that there are many pockets of success, just like his business.

As a businessperson, he's dead set against the intrusion of government into industry in the form of takeovers and bailouts. He rankles at the thought of the government determining an executive's salary. He also believes in personal responsibility, so he sees no justice in bailouts. Each business and person should live with the natural market consequences of their decisions.

Greg and Dilynn are living the American dream, having started a business they may never have envisioned, but for which they were really in training their whole lives. The product kind of designed itself with the help of artistic ability, friends, and some shop owners. And now that they've built the product and worked through their development pains, Language Art stands on its own as one of the more successful products in an otherwise very crowded and weak gift shop retail market. In many ways, lifestyle and working environment goals predominated the couple's vision of what they wanted, and the product came along to enable that vision. It maybe not the way it's drawn up in business textbooks, but it has worked for Greg and Dilynn.

Language Art

KEYS TO SUCCESS:

- Don't be afraid to have dreams.
- When the opportunity to realize those dreams presents itself, seize it.
- Don't worry if everything isn't perfectly planned. Have faith in God and yourself that you will find the answers.
- Keep the business concept simple, and bootstrap your way to success.
- Use sound financial strategies to minimize risk. You don't have to beg for business or compromise if you have a good product or service.
- Create a buzz by getting good publicity.
- Delays in filling orders and a sense of scarcity can be a good thing sometimes.
- It might be best to just ignore your competition. Do what you do very well, and the rest will fall in place.
- Your hobby or passion can become a viable business. There is a way to create your business on your terms.

Contact information:

Language Art
Middlebury, IN 46540
574-202-8183
www.languageartonline.com
Greg Puckett, President
E-mail: signs@languageartonline.com

8) We Are Fam-i-ly

Das Dutchman Essenhaus

Das Dutchman Essenhaus is a funny name to most of us and would not make much sense to any of you unless you've eaten a family-style meal there, stayed at their hotel, or bought a pie from their huge bakery. If you've traveled to northern Indiana Amish Country, you will know about Das Essenhaus, or Essenhaus, as most around here refer to the place.

I interviewed Lance Miller, son of Bob and Sue Miller, the founders of Das Dutchman Essenhaus. He's one of the vice presidents in the business now, along with two of his brothers, a sister, and a brother-in-law who work for the company, which has become a real hospitality and food conglomerate. Today the impression is of a huge, highly successful restaurant with tentacles stretching throughout the United States. But the real story behind how the company started reveals how a family struggled against tough odds to build a venue that has become synonymous with northern Indiana.

Bob and Sue Miller were living in Ohio in the late '60s and had gotten into a restaurant business with Sue's father, Emmanuel Mullet, and a few other brothers. The restaurant was doing okay, but all knew they had to grow to support their families. Emmanuel actually spent most of his time as a horse trader and traveler to the Topeka/Shipshewana/Middlebury, Indiana area, because there were fantastic horse auctions which continue to this day. He came across a twenty-four-hour truck stop called The Curve Inn in Middlebury and ate a few meals there. He found out it was for sale and suggested Bob and Sue buy it. Within a few months, they were in business.

Now keep in mind that they had no money to start the business. Minimal savings from Emmanuel, Bob, Sue, and a brother or two became the capital. Middlebury has always been a tight community, and outsiders have to earn their respect. The local bank wasn't interested in their business, so they got a bank from Shipshewana to finance them. Every day they had to make the fifteen-mile drive to Shipshewana to make deposits instead of the one-mile ride to the local bank.

The restaurant was closed for a few weeks to clean up, paint, make some new menus, and put up some new signs. It opened in January of 1971 with 120 seats and a few new Amish and Mennonite employees. Bob and Sue couldn't afford a house, so they had a single-wide mobile home in the parking lot. At the time, they had two daughters, and Lance was on the way. He was born in early April. Within two months, Sue was pregnant again. The doctor knew she was having twins, but didn't tell her until the third trimester because he was convinced she wouldn't be able to deal with that news so soon after the restaurant opened and Lance was born. Bob and Sue worked in the restaurant day and night. Sue would take Lance in his baby carrier and set him on the floor while she cooked at lunchtime. The twins, Joel and Jeff, were born in late March of 1972. For quite a while, all seven family members lived in the single-wide.

Das Dutchman Essenhaus is from the Pennsylvania Dutch language spoken by the Amish in Pennsylvania, Ohio, and Indiana. It translates as "The Dutchman Eatinghouse," and it definitely ties to the local Amish and Mennonite population. At the core, Das Essenhaus has built its reputation on the restaurant, which is best known for family-style meals of fried chicken, roast beef, noodles, gravy, stuffing, and more. Typically your meal will be topped off by one of their tremendous home-style pies, of which they have thirty or forty varieties available at any one time. The Dutch apple pie was served at the inauguration of Indiana governor Mitch Daniels and has been served twice at the request of Indiana senator Richard Lugar at events in Washington, D.C. featuring foods from throughout the country.

To get an idea of what Das Essenhaus has become in less than forty years, here's a snapshot of their present operation:

In Middlebury:

- Family restaurant seating 1,100 with attached full-service bakery
- Inn and conference center with eighty-nine hotel rooms and meeting space for up to 300
- Essenhaus Catering
- Village Gift Shops (seven shops)
- Dawdy Haus Inn—a small Amish home renovated as a bed and breakfast with seven rooms
- Essenhaus Foods, producing wholesale noodles, canned meats, salad dressings, and more. The noodles are available in grocery stores throughout the U.S. (A completely new, state-of-the-art noodle factory was opened in January of 2008.)
- Miniature golf
- Carriage rides

In Ohio:

- Der Dutchman Restaurants in Plain City, Walnut Creek, and Waynesville
- Dutch Village Restaurant in Sugarcreek
- Der Dutchman Countryside Hotel
- Dutch Creek Foods
- Dutch Valley Furniture
- Carlisle Inn at Sugarcreek and Walnut Creek

The Miller family in Middlebury owns most of the Indiana operations and about 50 percent of the Ohio operations.

When I asked Lance about the strategy behind the Amish-style restaurants, he said it really doesn't have anything to do with a marketing concept. He referred consistently to their vision, "A pleasant surprise in the country," and their mission, "Dedicated to providing each guest with a wholesome environment, warm hospitality, outstanding service, and consistent quality." To achieve the goals they had and to be comfortable with the style of service and food quality, Bob and Sue looked to their Amish and Mennonite roots. Bob was raised in an Amish family until age eight when they converted to the conservative Mennonite religion, and Sue has always been Mennonite.

Over the years, Lance says they have had many failures, and the one thing that seems to be consistent when they analyze why is situations where they don't have a strong Amish or Mennonite employee base. So now they try to put their operations where they know they can attract a significant number of Amish and Mennonite staff. They are closed on Sundays and don't serve alcohol or tobacco.

While the sprawling facilities and multi-faceted operations all managed by an on-site corporate office may look like a sophisticated management machine, Lance says things are still very simple. There is no master strategic plan. Most new ventures they foray into are the result of responding to demand or an opportunity. They then ensure that what they are considering is consistent with their mission and values. So over the years, when the lines for meals were too long and out the door, they would add seats. Now the 1,100-seat restaurant is the largest in the state of Indiana. The hotel was added when they realized there was really nothing close by and so many tourists and bus groups were looking for accommodations that would allow them to spend more time on site.

Lance declined to give sales information, but says that they are holding up fairly well in the recession. Employment in the local operation peaks at around 450 in the summer. Some statistics to give an idea of the scope of the operation:

- On a busy day in the summer, the restaurant will serve around 7,000 guests.
- In a week, they use up to 4,800 chickens and 2,000 dozen eggs in the restaurant and bakery.
- The day before Thanksgiving, they will sell approximately 2,000 pies.
- The noodle factory makes up to 13.5 tons of noodles in one week.
- More than 1 million gift shop items are sold annually.

The Essenhaus Food noodle production is really an example of adapting to meet a need rather than a pre-determined growth strategy. A local family had produced noodles for Essenhaus for many years in a small metal building on their tiny farm. The owners came to retirement age and wanted to sell the business. The Miller family believed these noodles had a unique quality to them and were something that set Essenhaus apart. So they bought the noodle-making equipment and took over the few wholesale accounts the owners had. A small building on the Essenhaus ground was used for production, but distribution and sales were growing rapidly, so they built a 20,000-square-foot noodle factory in 2008. This sales base has been a real blessing, because the recession has caused people to eat out less. While the Essenhaus restaurant has experienced some of this decline, grocery store sales have increased, and relatively inexpensive foods like pasta have been some of the biggest growth segments of the industry.

Essenhaus is the prototypical family business. Bob and Sue are still very involved in the business on a regular basis, although they do take more time off to travel. On a typical Saturday evening, Bob can still be found seating guests, walking the dining room, and checking out the kitchen. One proud accomplishment is the many employees who have worked for Essenhaus for many years. Some waitresses have more than thirty-five years, and several management staff members started their careers working in the restaurant during high school. Lance also mentioned that 25 percent of the workforce is under eighteen, which is a source of pride for the company because they have the opportunity to give young people their first job experience.

Lance says they are very careful not to change anything in the restaurant, and the menu remains very similar to what it was when they opened in 1971. They rely heavily on their vendor relationships, many of which also date back to the early days. Nothing is ever changed without extensive testing, even for seemingly commodity items like sugar, because they want to make sure the taste, quality, and consistency of their food and products remains.

Marketing of all the Essenhaus operations is a huge task, and they strive to keep it new all the time. But they still live by Bob Miller's admonition, "The best marketing is a happy customer." Beyond this basic daily marketing tenet, there are many other facets:

- An extensive Web site describing the facilities and allowing visitors to purchase many of their products online: *www.essenhaus.com.* Lance says this is the third or fourth generation of the Web site, and they believe it needs to be redone. They use e-mail marketing to several mailing lists and aren't yet using social media such as Facebook and Twitter.
- Numerous ads in local newspapers, brochure distribution, and regional advertising in travel or upscale consumer magazines are placed throughout the year.
- Their sales staff interfaces with the local convention and visitor's bureau and also attends several tourism shows each year to recruit tour groups to visit Essenhaus and the area.

- There is an on-site "quilt garden," which is the first of its kind in the area and part of a local network of quilt gardens which visitors can observe. This has become a big draw for the area in the last few years. (A quilt garden is made of hundreds or thousands of flowers planted for the season in the shape of a quilt.)
- Thursday night Classic Car Cruise-Ins during the summer, drawing as many as 250 cars.
- This fall, a new dinner theater, joint ventured with a local theater group and the school across the road from the Essenhaus, which has a large auditorium for the performances.
- Many special interest events like quilt shows, girlfriends' getaway weekends, food shows, fashion shows, train shows, etc. The business is always finding new ways to keep its base of customers interested and draw more people to its venues.

The Miller family and Das Essenhaus are recognized as leaders in the local business community. As Lance surveys the current economic malaise, he feels that to an extent, the county has been sort of an innocent bystander of the financial meltdown and soaring gas prices. While he favors more business diversification in the county, he's not quick to assign blame. The way he sees it, the county had a lot of success with the RV industry, and it was understandable they would ride that wave.

In the state of Indiana, Lance is a supporter of Mitch Daniels and generally favors his conservative economic policies which are consistent with the Miller family approach. He applauds Mitch for taking on tough issues and not bowing to political pressure. However, Lance questions cuts in tourism budgets statewide, as he sees tourism as one of the county's growing industries which brings a lot of dollars into the state. Lance and others at Essenhaus have been active in tourism leadership statewide and also the local economic development efforts.

While Lance sees President Obama as sort of a "rock star" who is very articulate and has a likable personality, he is very concerned about the administration's policies. He thinks some of the financial interventions during the fall of 2008 may have been necessary and is not at all convinced that the massive stimulus package and takeover of auto companies were good decisions. Projecting forward, he can't see how these policies will work, but is optimistic that we will find solutions to our problems and get back on the right track.

As Das Dutchman Essenhaus looks to its fortieth anniversary in a couple years, there is extreme pride in the Miller family about what Bob and Sue envisioned and how the business has played out. Their primary goal has always been to take care of each customer with the Amish and Mennonite spirit of hospitality, and they know they have succeeded. There are no grand plans, but Lance and his brothers and sisters relish the opportunity to build on the legacy of their parents so that the "pleasant surprise in the country" will remain a cornerstone of Elkhart County.

Das Dutchman Essenhaus

KEYS TO SUCCESS:

- Know that your faith in God and a service mentality can be pillars of your business approach.
- Realize that there is no substitute for hard work.
- Remember Bob Miller's words, "The best marketing is a happy customer."
- Develop great partnerships with your vendors and other related organizations. These partnerships become a key strategic asset.
- Remember that great food and warm hospitality are givens in the restaurant industry.
- Know that smoke and mirrors marketing can't make up for the reverse.
- Adapting to the times, spotting opportunity, and responding to both internal and external demand can be a business plan.
- Be very cautious in changing your basic concept—in every respect.
- Realize that quality and value imply not cutting corners. Add value and create a surprise for your customers.

Contact Information:

Essenhaus, Inc.
240 U. S. 20
P.O. Box 1217
Middlebury, IN 46540
Lance K. Miller, Vice President of Operations/CFO
Phone: 574.822.1262
E-mail: lance@essenhaus.com
www.essenhaus.com

9) Victims Need Not Apply

AE Techron

It was 1991, and Larry Shank had just completed what he thought was a successful year at Crown International. He had taken a product line from virtually zero profit to sales of more than $1 million in a few short years, and he was pretty pleased with himself. Larry was the type to notice things that didn't make sense to him and was quick to let his boss and others know what he thought would make the situation work better. Apparently management wasn't pleased with Larry's willingness to share his insights, so they gave him an opportunity to leave.

So just a few months after being married and draining his bank account for the wedding and honeymoon, Larry was forced to let his wife know the situation. He started some half-hearted attempts to find a job, but he knew what the real answer was. He wasn't a good employee and needed to run the show. Through his networking, he found out about an electrical component that one of the local companies had significantly overstocked. They were looking for a way to move the product, which was similar to the amplifiers and speaker systems Larry had been selling at Crown. So Larry bootstrapped a way to buy the product and sell it to a consumer market niche the company hadn't considered. His new company was born, initially financed almost entirely on credit cards.

Most of Larry's work at Crown had been business-to-business (B2B), and he was now focused on the consumer audio and sound market—amplifiers, speakers, etc. that would be sold at wholesale. Larry and his wife started running the business and eventually had a few employees. It was a constant struggle, but somehow they paid the bills and gradually grew the sales. In 1999, Larry stated that sales were $300,000, and between him and his wife, they took a combined salary of $15,000 from the business. He was starting to think he might need to look for a real job.

Larry had maintained a good relationship with several of his friends at Crown, and in January of 2000, he found out that Crown had been acquired by a large international company. One of the divisions, AE Techron, had a decent product line, but had lost the one customer who accounted for more than 90 percent of the sales. So the division was for sale, and Larry was able to craft a good deal to buy it. This division operated in the B2B space, and Larry thought that could complement his consumer business. A few highly skilled engineers and manufacturing talent came along to join Larry.

A few months later, Larry had the revelation that would change everything for him. He was on the phone, talking to one of his retail customers who was negotiating a price for an $18 item. The guy said that a Chinese company could make it for twenty-seven cents less, and he wanted Larry to cave on his price. A few minutes later, a potential customer called about an industrial speaker system, and Larry was explaining the product options to him. Larry gave him the price for the standard model but mentioned that the upgraded version which was $600 more. The guy took the higher priced version—no questions asked. At that moment, Larry knew that competing in the consumer-based commodity market against Chinese companies was not his future. All his efforts were poured into the industrial market, which is now 95 percent of his business.

AE Techron designs, manufactures, and sells power amplification and speaker systems for research companies, universities, the healthcare industry, and the military. The company is still a small company with around eighteen employees, many of whom have strong engineering training. Most of the products are very low volume, with some being single custom products. Price points range from a few thousand dollars to more than $100,000. Many of the customers have PhDs or are engineers, so the sales approach is highly technical. Because of the uses, the tolerance of the products must be extreme with respect to failure rates, exposure to elements, and high and low temperatures. More than the physical product, AE Techron sells engineering and reliability.

Larry was born and raised in Elkhart. His father was a state representative and had been his landlord until Larry bought the building from him a few years ago. Larry has strong ties to the community and is quite family-oriented.

What Larry loves about his business is that it can make a quality product and not obsess over every penny of production cost. Relatively good margins are possible, because customers know only a few companies can compete in these small markets. However, these small markets become one of Larry's main marketing challenges, because they are not readily identifiable and are not easy to sell to. Because of the technical nature of the products and the potential uses, the sales, design, and planning cycle can be two or three years. AE Techron doesn't really have a sales force. Most communication with customers is over the phone. Often major customers are flown in for design or testing meetings in the 15,000-square-foot plant.

Interestingly, the major source of new sales leads has become the Internet. Larry's theory is that his potential customers are Web-savvy and will do Internet searches to find him, so he does a lot of pay-per-click advertising to ensure people come to his site. The company's Web site itself is constantly evolving, but is quite technical and reads more like a product manual. Various calculators and formulas are built into the site so that Larry and other in-house staff can talk the potential customer through specifications and how the product might meet their needs. Only two brochures have been requested in the last few years, as everything is available on the Web site.

The nature of the one-off type of business and intermittent sales has proven profitable, but it also contributes to peaks and valleys. Another marketing challenge is finding customers who purchase some of Techron's current or new products on a more consistent basis. A few customers of this type have been identified, and Larry foresees sales rising drastically in the next few years. Both 2008 and 2009 will have sales in the $2 million range, while Larry can project sales growth of more than 30 percent in the next two years based on quotes and contracts that are coming in right now.

At this point, Larry feels the company is starting to move from the initial entrepreneurial stage to a stage where there will need to be more structure, management, and systems. There is a great spirit of teamwork in the building, and those who work there enjoy the ability to create and really contribute to the products going out the door. But to enable increased volume, Larry stays up at night wondering where the engineering talent will come from and how he will keep the pipeline going. Over the years, he has strategically reinvested his profits in human resources and has a lot of pride in the talent he has assembled. His top engineers have great credentials but can only design so much. At the product engineer and manufacturing technician level, Larry finds it difficult to recruit the people he needs. Last year he hired a graduating college engineer at a salary of just under $40,000, which is quite competitive in this market. After six months of training, he left for a job with Motorola in Chicago at a salary of $65,000.

So Larry is working on the next generation of AE Techron. He hired a sales manager last year to relieve his own workload in that area. Larry has always been the main sales guy. The week I interviewed him, he had just hired another engineer. But he knows he needs to tell the AE Techron story better if he wants to attract more people to his team. His goal is to find team members who are excited about the opportunity to be part of a company that is constantly changing. And he realizes he needs to pull himself out of the day-to-day to focus on strategic priorities like identifying the right market niches and determining new marketing strategies that go beyond the Internet.

The company really flies under the local radar, as 99 percent of sales are to companies outside of Indiana, and more than 30 percent of sales are international. There is little local advertising. So Larry was a little surprised when the local chamber of commerce approached him to appear in March of 2009 on the Huckabee show featured on Fox News. Former presidential candidate Mike Huckabee came to showcase the story of Elkhart, which had received a lot of attention due to the problems of the RV industry. Larry was featured on the show as someone growing a high-tech business—unlike the RV industry, which is mostly a lower-tech, assembly-type operation. Larry spoke to Huckabee about one of his products that is used to simulate lightning strikes on aircraft.

Because of Larry's political awareness from being the son of a legislator and also because of his business acumen, he is able to offer a relatively unique perspective on the current situation. He has respect for local and state legislators and believes they are well-intentioned. However, he doesn't believe they really understand the potential of high-tech businesses like his and is concerned that they will pursue traditional auto- or RV-related companies instead of spending time recruiting and encouraging businesses like his. He went out of his way to praise Governor Mitch Daniels and says he "gets it" with respect to how to attract new business. Larry was intrigued by Mitch's stated goal of recruiting and retaining company headquarters, because that's where their loyalties stay in times of trouble.

Larry sees the RV industry as being a great growth area in the past and very profitable, so he can understand why those in the county loved it. However, he sees the future in businesses like his—focused on a smaller niche—which will be more immune from cycles and also better able to use local talent. He believes companies like this can focus on quality and make a good profit, plus he sees them as more committed to living and working in the community.

His view of what's happening on a national basis is that it's frightening but understandable, given the background of the new president, who has always favored government solutions to problems. Larry's belief is that government doesn't run anything well—but even if they did, we don't have the money to do what they want to do. Larry is upset at the way that Elkhart County has been portrayed, which he thinks is as a victim which needs to be bailed out. He says that's not what the county is about and that his message to the Huckabee folks was to check back in about a year and they'll see real progress induced by the people of Elkhart County. Larry's attitude is that government officials often see their role as finding a way to fix problems for its people, but Larry says Elkhart County's message is, "Just get out of our way, and we'll find a solution."

In Larry's business life, he's never played the victim and decisively approaches challenges as just that. At the darkest times—when he lost his job or when his company was on the brink of failure—he has just kept looking for answers and found them in new markets and niche opportunities ignored by other companies. He envisions that same opportunity for others who may be struggling right now and is optimistic this will lead to a real comeback for the Elkhart region.

AE Techron

KEYS TO SUCCESS:

- When life throws you a curve ball, just pick yourself up and find a new path.
- In a tech business, you have to invest in really good people. Build your business around these people.
- Find a niche that doesn't focus on pennies so you can afford to provide an excellent product.
- The leader needs to know when it's time to move from everything revolving around them to surrounding themselves with good people motivated to do a good job.
- Build a great team and offer an opportunity to be creative, and you can attract real talent.
- The internet allows even small companies to have a truly international presence and can be a great selling platform.
- Don't whine; don't be a victim. It doesn't get you anywhere.

Contact Information:

AE Techron, Inc.
2507 Warren St.
Elkhart, IN 46516
Larry Shank, President and CEO
Phone: 574.295.9495
E-mail: lshank@aetechron.com
www.aetechron.com

10) RV Niche Company Still Going Strong

Kropf Industries, Inc.

The RV industry has been in a funk for several years, with a major decline in 2001, a few growth years thereafter, some flat years, a decline of 10 percent in 2007, and then the bottom dropping out in 2008 when sales were down 33 percent. Elkhart County is the RV capital of the world, so it's been hit hard—as documented elsewhere. But I heard about one company that has been fairly impervious to the decline. Kropf Industries of Goshen has found a niche and has been able to weather the storm by sticking to it. And the niche they found hasn't always been their sweet spot. They found it by necessity when they went through similar crises in the '70s and '80s.

Recreational Vehicles weren't prevalent in the 1940s, although the industry was starting to blossom. Solomon Kropf was a Goshen farmer and loved camping. On a vacation, he saw an RV and fell in love with it—the only problem was that he couldn't afford the price tag at the time. But he was a resourceful guy and came back to his farm and built a camper trailer for himself in his barn. He had it parked outside on State Road 15 when a dealer from Michigan happened by and asked if he could purchase it. When he found that Solomon had built it himself, he told him he could sell all that Solomon could manufacture, so a business was started.

Over the next several years, Solomon moved from farming to his new occupation as the owner of Kropf Industries. The company dabbled in RVs and manufactured homes, always with the intent of being on the cutting edge with new model designs, high quality workmanship, and custom built units. That formula served them well for the '50s and '60s, and the small company developed a solid reputation with steady increases in sales. In 1962, the farm building burnt to the ground, but they were back in production in a few months at a rented facility, with a new building complete within a year. That building is still part of the plant today.

Solomon's two sons, Bob and Vern, joined the company during that period, and in 1964, Vern moved to Florida to open an RV dealership that focused on Kropf products but also carried competitors' products. This strategy proved to be a key to the company's future success. The dealership opened during the time that mobile home parks were sprouting up in Florida. People who had fought World War II and the Korean War were starting to retire in Florida, so Vern Kropf had a good thing going and was able to monitor the market.

In the early 1970s, the industry experienced the gas crisis, which affected RV and mobile home shipments dramatically. Then in the late '70s, we had the Jimmy Carter recession with high inflation and high interest rates. RV shipments actually declined by almost 50 percent in 1979 and 1980, taking total industry shipments down from 390,000 units to 107,000 units. Bob and Vern had purchased the business from their father in 1976, and now they were wondering how to survive.

Other factors had affected Kropf during this period. The company had always maintained its strategy of building high-end products, but many bigger companies had come into the burgeoning market offering lower-quality, lower-priced RVs and manufactured homes. Kropf tried a few times to get down and dirty with that market, but failed. Luckily, Solomon (before he retired in '76), Bob, and Vern had started to notice a new type of RV that was becoming very popular in Florida and other retirement areas.

The units were called recreational park trailers and were a cross between an RV and manufactured home. Because recreational park trailers are transportable and built on a trailer chassis, they are classified as RVs. However, they are meant to be put semi-permanently in a campground-style park, where they usually become seasonal homes for retirees. Today the standards are that park models cannot exceed 400 square feet. The units are delivered ready to hook up to utilities and have a full kitchen, bathroom, bedroom, and small living space. Many have lofts to add a little room, and some have slide-out walls that can expand the space even further. When set in an RV park or resort, the owner has an instant home. They can either purchase the lot or rent it on a yearly basis.

What the company found out about this market was that it was relatively small but growing. To give you a feel, today these small vacation homes can be purchased from about $40,000 to $60,000. And staying true to their quality strategy, the company focused on the high end of the market. During the next ten to twenty years, Kropf found a ready market in Sunbelt areas. Kropf became known as the custom builder to the park trailer market, working through RV dealers and campgrounds to sell their units. In fact, they abandoned all other RVs and manufactured homes and now focus exclusively on recreational park trailers.

The third generation took over Kropf when Don Kropf (Bob's son) and Curt Yoder (Don's brother-in-law) purchased the business from Bob and Vern about twelve years ago. They are fifty-fifty owners, and both sat down for the interview with me.

Don, who is fifty-two, joined the family business right out of high school, and it's all he's ever done. Curt, forty-eight, worked in the plant during high school and college and met his wife, Sheri (Kropf), during that time. Don is the plant manager and stays close to home. Curt is the sales manager and has one other salesman working for him. The two of them call on the dealers and attend trade shows. Sheri actually works in the front office and helps a lot with decorating, colors, and finishes for the new models. The day I was there, she was decorating a new park model trailer for shipment to a big industry trade show coming up in a few weeks.

The recreational park trailer component of the RV industry is relatively small—less than 5 percent. Curt is President of the industry trade association, Recreational Park Trailer Industry Association, Inc. (RPTIA), and says that the industry is down by about 55 percent in shipments. Kropf, however, is down by less than 15 percent and has kept its employment of about fifty relatively stable. Kropf really hasn't dropped prices and has maintained their production of five to six units per week. Yearly sales the last few years have been in the $11–12 million range with net profit margins of 7 to 9 percent. With the sales off a little, profits are still good and have only dropped about 2 percent.

Don and Curt attribute their ability to maintain reasonable volume during the downturn to several factors. First, they have noticed that much of the decline in volume industry-wide has happened in the Sunbelt ,and while that market had been strong for them in the past, competitive forces have moved them to more northern markets like New Jersey, Pennsylvania, Michigan, and Minnesota. Second, as in most recessions, the more affluent customer is still buying, and that is where Kropf has an advantage. Virtually every unit they produce has some customization, whereas most competitors focus on cookie-cutter models. Finally, the company has an excellent reputation for customer service and sales support. So while some competitors may be cutting back in this area, Curt and his team are redoubling their efforts to stay in touch with their dealer network with weekly or biweekly phone calls, sales trips, and trade shows high on their sales strategies. A functional Web site requires consumers to supply contact information, which Kropf follows up on by communication directly with the consumer and also passing on the lead to the nearest dealer.

The 52,000-square-foot plant is a model of efficiency, with the same basic production line being in place since the early '70s. A unit begins with a trailer chassis and moves through ten stations to eventual completion. One key to a reasonable cost structure is relatively low labor costs compared to the rest of the industry. While this may seem counterintuitive to the quality mantra at Kropf, it works for a few reasons. The first is that their workforce knows that they will have steady work all year long. The RV industry, even in the best of times, can become very seasonal, with many forced layoffs throughout the year. Also, the industry became known for mass producing the RVs to the point that workers had very menial jobs like installing one towel bar all day long, with a piece rate bonus mentality. So the work can be boring at a very fast pace. At Kropf, with the emphasis on quality and customization, Don expects his workforce to be more versatile, which contributes to a better job situation, and the pace is steadier to ensure quality.

Kropf also has its own in-house cabinet and countertop shop. There are two seamstresses who produce their curtains and drapes. Most RV companies of Kropf's size purchase these items. Kropf is able to control quality and cost for these components.

With Curt being is in a leadership position in the industry (following Don's dad, Bob, who was one of the founders of RPTIA) and with the number of friends both Curt and Don have in the industry, I was able to get an insider perspective of how the RV business got to where it is and what the challenges are now. Curt's opinion is that the industry and its financing partners lost their sense of reality, making loans to consumers who weren't qualified to buy. This situation was further exacerbated by lenders who were very lenient with dealer floorplan financing (loans to finance the inventory of RV units on stock in dealers' showrooms).

They got sloppy with lending standards and allowed dealers to get behind on payments, but once everything went bad last year, the reaction was swift and swung in the opposite direction, with financing virtually impossible to get now, even for qualified consumers and solid dealers. Another observation was that some RV manufacturers got a "quick buck disease" when they observed all the larger companies buying up the smaller ones. They were trying to build their sales and cut corners doing so, sometimes forcing dealers to take more inventory than was needed. Some entrepreneurs started new companies to build them quickly with the intent of making a quick profit on selling the operation, as opposed to solid companies like Kropf who have been around for more than sixty years. Curt and Don have continued a legacy of conservative financial strategy with low borrowing and emphasis on watching their margins all the time.

Having lived through tough times in the past, Curt and Don are confident the industry will come back. Don said he's not happy about how the press has overblown the situation in Elkhart County, making it appear that it is in need of relief analogous to the situation with Katrina. Curt said that Midwest values are that a community takes care of its own, and it is up to the task.

Both believe state and local political leaders are doing their best and are advocates for the industry. But they aren't so sure about national leaders. They were disturbed by the visits by the president to our area and wondered out loud what he really talked about that would provide true relief. Don mentioned that we don't need more road projects or airport runway additions now. What we need is a solid economy, which had been neglected by the Bush administration, but there is grave concern that runaway spending can't and won't help. They suggest that one thing that would help is to provide incentives for financial institutions to start lending again to RV consumers and dealers. Curt also mentioned a supposed recent enhancement to the Small Business Administration (SBA) loan program, but he's not aware of one loan that has been made, and his understanding is that the banks don't even know how to make the program work.

Don and Curt are proud businessmen, having carried the legacy of Don's grandfather to this generation. Don especially is proud that the Kropf name has carried on. Since they bought the business from Bob and Vern, there has been a string of profits virtually every month. The business has provided good income to three generations of their family and to hundreds of employees. The joy and challenge of that legacy is what keeps them going.

The family legacy may be coming to an end. Neither have children who have indicated a desire or penchant for the business. And both Don and Curt made it obvious that they don't intend to die in the saddle. So they look to the next five to ten years as their time to continue the tradition, but also to start to look at selling the company. After what they've accomplished, one can only hope the industry comes back to the point that others will realize the gem that has been created for a potential new owner.

Kropf Industries, Inc.

KEYS TO SUCCESS:

- Find a niche that you can exploit.
- Stick to what you do best.
- Know that leadership and a solid reputation in your industry can pay off in the long term.
- Employees aren't necessarily interested in the quick buck—provide stability and a rewarding job environment, and you can ensure their loyalty.
- Realize that it's tough to carry a family legacy for too many generations, especially when children observe the challenges entrepreneurs face each day.
- Don't discount the value of selling to the more affluent market; there is always money available for quality products.
- Instead of cashing in or giving up, work even harder in tough times. You will be stronger for the next challenge.

Contact information:

Kropf Industries, Inc.
58647 S. R. 15
P.O. Box 30
Goshen, IN 46527-0030
Phone: 574.533.2171
Toll-free: 800.634.2171
www.kropfind.com
Don Kropf, President
E-mail: don@kropfind.com
Curt Yoder, Vice President
E-mail: curt@kropfind.com

11) An Amish Business Thriving in a Modern World

A&R Machine Shop

While all the stories about the companies in this book are extremely compelling, it is possible this one will amaze you the most. A&R Machine Shop may sound like a small business, but when I tell you it is owned by the Amish, you might be thinking it's even smaller. Let me tell you that this Amish shop can compete with virtually any machine shop or steel fabricator in the U.S., and they generate their own power, are self-taught, have no computers, do all their drawings freehand, and have no Web site and no e-mail. Would it also surprise you if I told you they have achieved ISO-9000 certification? (ISO-9000 is a rigorous international quality program required by most major manufacturers in order to be a supplier.)

First State Bank of Middlebury, featured elsewhere in this book, told me about A&R. For a few weeks I tried to find it, because the shop is located in a very rural area between Goshen and Middlebury. Finally I determined where it was and stopped one afternoon. I found a sign on the road that led to a large white building behind a farmhouse and a few outbuildings. Upon entering the front shop, I met a few Amish men, and I asked for Delbert Miller, who was the person I was told to talk with. I was told Delbert wasn't there but I could wait to speak with his brother Wayne. While waiting for about fifteen minutes, I made a few observations. First, the men seemed very friendly but quite busy. The front area was dark, with little lighting. I could hear the sound of machinery behind some doors leading to the shop area. And I could hear a meeting going on as the men spoke in Pennsylvania Dutch. Wilbur soon exited the meeting and greeted me. I told him that the bank president had suggested I contact Delbert and that I was writing a book about businesses in Elkhart County. He took my business card and told me Delbert was on the road and would call me later in the day. (Some Amish use cell phones, especially for business situations. A&R actually has a landline phone and in addition Delbert is able to borrow his driver's cell phone.)

Later that day, I spoke with Delbert, and he said he was reluctant to talk about their business because it is not the Amish way to brag about what they do. But he could see the benefit in telling others how they operate and thought the theme of the book might help some others in their lives or business. We agreed to meet a few days later.

Delbert began by giving me the one piece of sales literature they have, which is a four-page brochure with several pictures of items they have manufactured from steel. I later found that the brochure is relatively recent and a response to the downturn in sales over the last year or so. This is the first time they've really had to market themselves.

Delbert's father, Rudy Miller, was a self-taught welder who did miscellaneous welding and horseshoeing in the '50s and '60s. When times got a little tough, Rudy took a job in a boat manufacturing plant, where he learned more about steel fabrication and machining. His brother-in-law, Abe Yoder, was a skilled engine mechanic who moved up from the Fort Wayne area around 1969 to collaborate on the new A&R Machine Shop. Rudy had eight children, and Abe had several kids also. The business started to grow, primarily by reputation for quality work.

By the end of the first year, Rudy gave up the horseshoeing to focus on A&R. As the company grew, there was a steady supply of new workers from sons and nephews. Delbert was the oldest Miller son and started working there in 1974 at the age of seventeen. The Amish go to school until eighth grade, which means they are about fourteen or fifteen years old. Delbert had already worked a few years in an RV factory but had been laid off, so Rudy asked him to join the family business.

They were operating out of a small building that had been built on their farm and were starting to burst at the seams. So they went to Elkhart County officials asking to add on to the structure and were denied. Sometime in the mid-'80s, purely as a reason to accommodate the growth, Abe started his own engine business just down the road, called Yoder & Sons Mechanical, which still operates today. The two businesses often collaborate or refer business to each other. Rudy and the Miller sons kept the machine shop and steel fabrication and now had room to grow that business.

Steadily the business continued to grow, and the complexity of work also increased. They were getting into bigger jobs, requiring more lathes, cutting machines, cranes, steel storage, welding equipment, and more. In the late '90s, they were again at a crossroad—expand their building or lay off some people and saddle their growth. In fact, Delbert had even started one little side business that required custom equipment to manufacture some specialty rollers and vinyl sleeves for RV slide-outs. Because their present facility couldn't handle this business, he bought the equipment himself and installed it in a barn by his own home a mile or so down the road. He and his sons worked on these products on the side and didn't move that business back into the main plant until his sons started to reach plant working age of about sixteen. (The Amish have exemptions allowing some of their younger children to work in family businesses.)

In any event, they were now faced with approaching the County again. They were told the only way they would approve any expansion was if a totally new building was constructed, complying with all zoning and design standards. The family agreed to take on this challenge, and in 2001 a new 34,000 square foot facility was built.

The story of how this was financed is amazing to me as an entrepreneur who has always fought the battles of having enough capital to achieve my needs. There were six partners at the time—Rudy, Delbert, Wayne, and three brothers-in-law. They hired an outside design firm, which came up with the construction cost. Delbert declined to elaborate on the cost of the building, although it's pretty easy to determine that it is probably in the $1 to $2 million range. About a year before the start of construction and during the construction period, the owners didn't take their normal withdrawals of profits from the business. That became their equity of approximately 45 percent of the total cost. The remaining 55 percent was borrowed from First State Bank, and that amount was repaid in three years!

To understand what A&R does, know that virtually every product is custom made. Many are small metal parts, scaffolds, mezzanines, racks, cages, etc. that are a one-time fabrication. As an example, a mezzanine, which is one of their specialties, can be made to be the second floor of a large plant and to hold thousands of pounds of equipment and many people. The cost can exceed $100,000. It is fabricated in their shop and shipped by common carrier to the client. The beams are large enough that cranes are necessary to carry them. A&R will often then send their workers to the customer site to assemble the various beams, catwalks, etc.

They can also make tanks, trailers, rollers, and more that will have a specific design needed by the customer. After prototypes are produced and the specifications are agreed to, these can be repetitive products that are produced for years that may go into autos, RVs, tractors, or similar products.

I was honored to have a plant tour with Delbert. The main shop is very open, with several large lathes and cutting machines. A large mezzanine provides a second story in the plant where some specialty products are manufactured. The plant is noisy with several Amish hard at work. The day I was there, they had just completed several wood-burning boiler furnaces, and there was a large tanker truck being retrofitted to function as a manure hauler. Large skylights provide most of the lighting, but there are also propane-powered lights. One or two large cranes were also in use.

One amazing example of their creativity is a large cage in the middle of the plant. My understanding is that the various lathes require press brake dies (metal bars) to adapt to various machining techniques. These bars are about twelve feet long and are quite heavy. In the past, these were stored on the shop floor on large carts that got in the way. The plant is about fifty feet high at its apex, and this cage was built there, with a large carousel system inside (the shelves of the carousel are horizontal to the floor and the carousel rotates up and down). With hydraulic pressure and buttons, they are able to advance the carousel to choose the bar they need and then pull it out through a small door that is the length of the cage. Admittedly, I am not an engineer and haven't seen many plants, but I have never seen anything like this. It was totally designed by Delbert and his co-workers and is featured in their brochure. He told me they've sold similar systems to other plants.

Another aspect of the plant to keep in mind is that they are totally self-sufficient with respect to power generation. They are not even connected to the power grid. Instead, their main source of power is a John Deere 500-horsepower diesel engine. Approximately 500 gallons of diesel fuel are used per week, and this engine powers their hydraulic pumps for most of their machines—plus it provides any electricity by use of generators. I also observed a very interesting heating system. Imagine how much heat the diesel engine gives off. The engine sits in a small room with a few other pieces of equipment. The heat from this room is drawn into a series of fans and filters which take the hot air to the top of the plant, and the hot air is then forced through two long four- or five-foot round ducts the length of the plant. This becomes the main heating source. Another large return air duct is in the center top of the plant and draws in the heat from the machines, recycles it, and filters it to be moved through the same system again. When the diesel engine is not running, there is another hot water heating system in the plant floor, which can be powered by a bank of approximately forty auto-style batteries that are constantly recharged by generators and can power the plant for four or five days when it is not in production. The heating system was designed by a local contractor with input from A&R and constructed by Honeyville Metals in Topeka, Indiana. Delbert believes similar systems have now been sold by Honeyville to other plants.

The process of how a product is developed is interesting. Delbert spends about 50 percent of his time on the road going to plants of customers to see what they might need, most of the time after they have called him with a specific request. He is driven by an "English" driver to the plants. (The Amish don't use automobiles and travel by buggy themselves. Non-Amish people are called "English" by the Amish.) At the site, Delbert talks to the customer and reviews any of their drawings to determine what they really need. Often it's something to improve efficiency in a plant, mechanize a production step, or provide storage or space. Delbert offers various suggestions based on his vast experience and then makes a rough sketch of the proposed solution. That sketch and Delbert's notes come back with him to the plant, where he starts working with his nephew, who is a more skilled drawer and also is able to estimate the cost of the job. I reviewed several of the drawings, and they are done on plain, white letter-sized paper, freehand. They are not drawn to scale, but have many measurements and specs on them. In some cases they have engineering drawings prepared by the customer or an outside engineer or architect. All the information is assembled and the customer is given a quote.

Once the project is approved, a document called the "Shop Traveler" is prepared to include a copy of the quote, drawings, and production steps. This accompanies the product through the plant to give the workers the specifications for what they are making and cutting, what materials are needed, etc.

While a large part of their business is close to home, they have customers in many other states. Delbert told me an interesting story of a job for a company in Sacramento, California. A man working there had been in the Midwest and was aware of A&R. They had a need for a large scaffolding or mezzanine system in their plant, and there were some unusual engineering challenges with the project. He asked several steel fabricators in California to quote the job, and they all said it wasn't possible to do what he wanted. Knowing he had seen a very similar solution done by A&R where he previously worked, he sent the specs to Delbert. The job was quoted, and the company agreed to it. A&R fabricated the components and shipped them to California. Five of the A&R partners and their wives then took a two-week trip to California with their driver. They spent two days installing the product in the plant and used the rest of the time to visit San Francisco, see the redwood forests, and witness the Pacific Ocean.

In 2008, Rudy Miller, the founder and patriarch of the family, died. As I sat in the office interviewing Delbert, there was a large collection of rifles and shotguns displayed. Rudy loved guns and also loved his business. Delbert and the others I talked with display a very quiet confidence that comes from knowing they do high quality work and can tackle almost any challenge. Whether it's just the Amish way or Rudy's guiding hand, Delbert wanted me to know that honesty was a cornerstone of their business philosophy. They stress quality and never cut corners, believing that this philosophy is essential to long-term success.

Now that Rudy is gone, his wife is a partner in the business with the other six main partners. A few years ago, they sold some stock to twelve of the nephews and sons who were more interested in the business and working there. Each was allowed to purchase 2 percent, and they are considered silent partners. The main six partners meet monthly to review safety reports, human resource issues, new customers, projects, finances, new equipment, and more. A few days after the meeting, there is a company-wide meeting with all the workers to update them on everything. This rigorous planning and communication with the workforce is often neglected in English businesses, in my own experience.

When I asked Delbert how many employees they have, he said, "None." What I found out is that all who work there and who are not the main partners are considered subcontractors. There are various legal reasons for this, and the arrangement has been reviewed and blessed by an English attorney. One of the factors is that the Amish are not required to pay Social Security taxes in their own businesses. Presumably each subcontractor has his own business and therefore avoids the tax.

At present there are thirty-two men working at the plant, down from a high of forty-two. Delbert declined to reveal sales, but says they are down about 25 percent from a year ago. The reduced staff has been primarily through attrition as some have started their own welding shops or moved to other opportunities. Only two were actually let go, and these were both workers where the owners felt there were work quality issues. Delbert said that in his thirty-plus years in the business, they have had only three people they have actually let go for performance reasons. There has never been a drug or theft problem in the business. Delbert also told me that one of the highlights of each year is a two-day trip for all the partners and workers with their wives or girlfriends (and of course, a few drivers). They have gone as far as Niagara Falls, but normally go to a state park. There are games, hiking, food, and fun. All expenses are paid, and the workers are paid for this time.

For the first time, Delbert and the partners are actually worried about getting some additional business to keep everyone busy. So Delbert is doing some prospecting, and as I mentioned, this is the reason for the new brochure. Delbert has been used to making his calls almost exclusively on customers who have asked him to come in for a specific need. Now he finds himself stopping by existing customers to see what he can do for them or actually cold prospecting. He really doesn't enjoy this, because the sales approach is not really the Amish way. They also sell through some English sales representatives, one of whom does a lot with the auto industry, so that business is down (A&R subcontracts for several Tier 1 suppliers to the auto industry).

The company is still profitable and has not even drawn on their available line of credit. They have had a few major customers go out of business, leaving some uncollectible debt. One major customer is several months behind right now, and they have worked out a COD arrangement for new orders with a partial payment on the account receivable. Delbert believes this is necessary in tough times and can help preserve a good company. He said they are sitting on more than $300,000 of past-due receivables right now. On the other hand, their philosophy is to pay their vendors almost immediately, normally within one week, and they have continued that practice even now.

As mentioned, Delbert is reluctant to speak about keys to success in fear of appearing less than humble. But he said their philosophy is that all they achieve because the honor goes to the Lord. Their responsibility as workers is to make the best use of their time on a daily basis and have concern for their customers' needs. Competition is not nearly as overt as in the rest of the business world, from what I gathered. Their focus is on quality work in what they do, and they aren't concerned about competitors. In fact, Delbert told me there are eight small welding shops in the area operated by former workers at A&R, and while they may bid against each other on a few jobs, they also work together often.

At the end of our interview, I talked with Delbert about the political and economic situation. The Amish don't vote for religious reasons, but they have some awareness of what is happening. Delbert gets the local newspaper, but he says he rarely reads it, and he only reads the headlines when he does. The Amish don't watch TV or listen to the radio. Delbert is certainly aware of the economic downturn and knows the Elkhart area has been particularly hard hit. He said it's probably "good for us," because everyone had become spoiled and complacent thinking the business would always be there. He believes that's true for A&R, and they've had to adjust their thinking.

He doesn't spend much time thinking about what has happened and isn't about to get involved politically. Rather, he thinks the best he can do is accept what God has given us and pray for our leaders, which he does daily. He is aware of the large stimulus packages and bailouts and considers them to be a large waste of money. His belief is that our leaders are put in their place by God and derive their power from God, but whatever happens is God's will, even if it means we are headed to the Apocalypse.

So the motto for A& R Machine Shop is to keep doing what they've done for the last forty years and live by their simple philosophies: Do God's will, be honest in all your dealings, do quality work, have concern for your customers, and treat everyone well, because we are all creatures of God. Resilience is embodied in all of this, as you have to adapt to what God throws at you.

A&R Machine Shop

KEYS TO SUCCESS:

- Remember that all the honor in doing your work goes to the Lord.
- Have an abundance mentality—there is plenty of business to go around.
- Just focus on doing what you do best every day, and work hard at it.
- Know that innovation comes from many places and in many forms.
- Realize that formal education is not as important as common sense, experience, and ingenuity.
- Take what life and God gives you, and make the most of it.
- The leaders in all businesses need to stop to communicate, plan, and organize.
- Business leaders also need to communicate with the rest of the team and show them they appreciate what they do.
- Consider how you can simplify your life and your business.

Contact Information:

A&R Machine Shop
14719 C.R. 20
Middlebury, IN 46540
Phone: 574-825-5686
Fax: 574-825-4908
Delbert Miller, President

12) Some Final Thoughts

Why Real Recovery Now Seems Likely

As I wrap up this book in the early fall of 2009, I am now realizing that there is cause for real hope, but that there are also many challenges ahead. When I embarked on this journey to meet with businesses, I didn't know what I would really find. I knew how I felt about things, and I also thought I knew how I'd be approaching this if I ran a major business working through these times.

But the stories of how all these companies were founded, how they have responded to adversity, and how hard they are working today are very inspiring to me. I knew a little about some of these companies, but I am truly amazed at what they have accomplished, the challenges they've met, and what consistently genuine people are running these businesses. Of the companies approached for the book, only one company chose not to be featured. All the others were very welcoming and most forthright in telling me what was happening in their businesses. They spent much time with me and gave me good ideas for the book. All were very encouraging and shared that they wanted the real story of Elkhart County to be told. They agreed we weren't being portrayed correctly. They were also very clear about what scares them in the current political climate.

The optimism of the leaders featured in this book refueled me. Many of these companies started because of big dreams which founders weren't afraid to chase. Elkhart County is a religious area, and a faith in God and the goodness of men and women was consistently mentioned. Almost every business has experienced dramatic adversity, which has positioned them well to respond in the current times. Many are growing or gaining market share while other companies are struggling or folding.

Another thing I noticed was the lack of excessive ego with these men and women. While I considered what they have done to be extraordinary, they saw it as just doing what they do. Sure, I found great pride in their people and their companies. But mostly what I found was quiet confidence that they will be able to respond to whatever is thrown at them, and a sense that Elkhart County and our country will come back.

President Obama came again in early August to hand out some stimulus money for some companies looking to do some "green" projects. At this point, really no effect can be seen from the Stimulus Plan—at least not in our area. Whatever programs were supposedly targeted for the RV industry haven't trickled down. The economy is showing a few signs of recovery, but unemployment is even worse across the country. Many people have left Elkhart County, and at least some were probably illegal aliens previously drawn here by RV jobs. Recently the news has been much more balanced with new jobs announcements seeming to come more than stories of cutbacks or closings. The county's leaders allocated $350,000 in tax dollars to fund the Elkhart Economic Development Corporation, which has become even more active under the leadership of Dorinda Heiden-Guss and a committed board of directors. Some major announcements of new hybrid truck and car factories have been made, but actual operations are many months away, dependent on financing, incentive packages, acquiring space, and more. There is talk of wind turbines, solar panels, new biofuels, and similar green projects coming to the area. Tourism appears to be on an up-tick in our area, and the RV industry is showing signs of life, with some factories calling workers back or consolidating operations here.

The mood in the country seems to have changed. The month of August saw all the town hall meetings, primarily aimed at discussing the president's government-run healthcare program. The Card Check legislation and Cap and Trade are also top-of-mind. All of these struggles and discussions have put back into focus what our country is really all about. Many—including me—really weren't paying attention to how far away we have strayed from our country's founding beliefs. Many of us started to wake up a few years ago, but millions more have awoken in the last six months to find a country they don't really recognize.

There is still a massive political and cultural struggle, and many forces want to take us in a direction that could be catastrophic if you believe that the United States is the greatest country to ever grace the earth. Some who voted for Barack Obama remain entrenched with his views and refuse to acknowledge the dangers ahead. Others have full knowledge of what their agenda is and are moving at breakneck speed to implement radical change. A few political leaders are starting to realize they work for the people and that we don't really care how long they have been in office. If power is all they have to offer, we want them out. So we're being drawn to new leaders who get it—who understand what the battle really is and who are willing to fight for us. And we're repudiating the agenda of the Obama administration and his network of supporters.

So therein is my hope—hope that we've woken up, hope that we will return to our roots, and hope that we will continue to take care of our own without the government telling us we have to. Hope that we'll let businesses like the ones in this book do their thing and that government will get out of the way. Hope that there will still be an American dream. Hope that more of us will speak our minds and tell our friends and families why this is so important. I think this is real hope.

13) How to Boost Sales and Profits Now—Recession Rescue

Special Collection of Articles, Essays, Archive Materials, and Notes by Dan S. Kennedy

What follows is a collection of previously published essays, articles, blogs, weekly faxes (sent to Glazer-Kennedy Insider's Circle Diamond members), and other material related to prospering in un-prosperous times. At the end, The Plan, invites you to organize key ideas from these writings into action strategies of your own.

This book's author, John Cohoat, is a Certified No-B.S. Business Advisor for Glazer-Kennedy Insider's Circle and is trained by Dan and Bill Glazer. He is leading one of approximately one hundred local chapters of Glazer-Kennedy. John thanks Dan for offering to contribute his ideas on how to respond to the recession in this book.

John's chapter is in Northern Indiana and Southwest Michigan, and if you live in this area and would like to attend a chapter meeting for free, please visit *www.cohoatbusinessgrowth.com.* If you are interested in an opportunity to get more than $600 of free educational materials and strategic ideas for your business from Glazer-Kennedy Insider's Circle, you should review the Most Incredible Free Gift Ever on **page 145-146.**

INTRODUCTION

Happy New Year, No really seriously, I mean 2009, Happy!

When I was just getting my adult act together, finding my way out of high school and into business, the brothers of the girl I was dating, a dentist's daughter, worked as car parking valets at a local, upscale restaurant, called LANNINGS. Christmas Eve was a big night there, but New Years Eve was THE big night. People made reservations months in advance and made certain to arrive early because the bar was filled to SRO with vultures hoping for no-shows and unexpectedly available tables. For the record, New Years Eve rolls around here in northeastern Ohio in winter. Sometimes, by then, we are ears deep in snow and bitter cold. Other times, still mild weather, only pregnant with gloom and miserable weather to come. Other times, in the 40's instead of freezing, but besieged with rain-snow-sleet, ice, wind. The youngest of the two brothers, from whom I got my first business loan handed over by him in coffee cans of coins from under bed, told me that - even though they stood outside without cover in starched shirts and bow ties and unlined red jackets from 5:00 PM until 1:00 AM, and had to park 2/3rds of the cars in the empty office complex parking lot across the street, running back and forth all night, they hoped and prayed and dreamed of having the worst, most vile, most violent and nasty mix of rain, snow, sleet, wind and cold possible on New Years Eve. *Because when that happened, tips quadrupled.*

Of course, they were paying for the lion's share of their college educations, not expecting or getting them for free, so they were motivated. They had goals.

LANNINGS is still thriving. I went there a couple years back for New Years Eve. And the principle enunciated by the brothers-not-grim is also unchanged. The worst of weather makes opportunity quadruple for those willing to wade out into it and collect money.

I live in a place where there's a lot of weather. Carla is interested in the TV weather reports so when she's here we watch it on the 11:00 PM news. If I'm by myself, I never do. Never check it. Just like I never even think about the price of gas. Because I am going where I'm going and I'm going to do what I'm going to do regardless of the weather or the price of gas. I have NEVER let such things dictate to me. NEVER. Not in 1979, 1989, 1999 and not in 2009. I might add: entire societies or individuals *choose* their dictators. Which is why, so often, liberators are shocked to find themselves unwelcome - if they really wanted liberated, they'd be liberated.

Somebody thinks: well, it's easy for you not to let weather or gas prices dictate; you have a good, new 4-wheel drive car with good tires and you are rich. No. I am rich because when I had old, bad, rusty, leaky, falling-apart cars and bald tires and no money I still did not permit circumstances to dictate. I am, incidentally, speaking both literally *and* metaphorically, for those keeping score.

Anyway, happy, happy, happy New Year.

If You Want More, Make Yourself More Valuable

The mayor of a small town once wrote to Benjamin Franklin asking for a donation so the town could buy a bell for its town square. Franklin sent money with a note suggesting they forego the bell in favor of buying books for the town library. It is at the library we might find an answer to why so few succeed and why most fail – at anything, at everything.

Most people do not apply themselves to acquiring know-how nor apply the know-how they acquire. In short, they have the attention span of a gnat, the diligence of an idle, random breeze. They certainly don't *study.*

I have become quite rich and somewhat celebrated, reaching the pinnacle of success in not one but three different fields. At each required skill-set, I once sucked. For me, there has always been a crawl to competence, then a fast rise to superiority. Part of the process is getting through of a lot of information in a hurry but also continuously. For nearly 25 years, I read a book a day plus newspapers, trade journals, newsletters, visited the public library weekly; took on a needed skill and so thoroughly and intensely studied it as to become a world class expert. When I was teaching myself to be an advertising copywriter, for example, I studied no less than an hour everyday, listened to recorded material on the subject constantly, sought out and got to know the top people in the field, and when one told me to take great direct-response ads and write them out longhand 21 times each, to teach my subconscious the rhythm of such writing, I did that with 100 ads. I collected over 200 books on the subject and immersed myself in them. I built organized files of samples that fill a room. I traced one master back to his teachers, they to theirs, thus even knowing the genealogy of the field. When I am asked by fledgling or journeymen copywriters how they, too, might have clients waiting in line to pay them $100,000.00 fees when there are thousands of copywriters advertising their availability for 1/10th that or less, and I tell them this answer, they reject it. **They seek rewards out of kilter with their value and are unwilling to do what is necessary to build up their value.**

The same answer could be given by the top earners in insurance, real estate, retail store ownership, dentistry – name the business or profession. The answer is the same.

I am told by people all the time that they simply do not have time to read and listen to all the material they have purchased or subscribed to. But time is democratic and just. Everyone has the same amount. When I choose to read with my mid-morning coffee break and you choose to blather about trivia with friends; when I choose to study for an hour sitting on my backyard deck at day's end but you choose to watch a TIVO'd American Idol episode, we reveal much. When someone says he does not have the time to apply himself to acquiring the know-how required to create sufficient value for his stated desires, he is a farmer surrounded by ripe fruit and vegetables, whole grains and a herd of cattle on his own property who dies of starvation, unable to organize his time and discipline himself to eat.

Incidentally, success in every business, including yours, depends on *mastery* of a handful of critical competencies (one of which is always marketing). The individual who sets out earnestly and diligently to acquire a wealth of know-how in each winds up with wealth in his bank account. All others watch with envy and cry in their soup, two activities they do seem *to* find time for.

It Your Income's Not Where You Want It There's A Reason

One of my earliest mentors had his office walls adorned top to bottom, side to side, with big, handwritten signs intended as cautions to others as well as reminders for himself. If you've ever been in a direct sales environment, you've probably seen such a place. Two of the biggest signs read "Thumb-Suckers Not Welcome Here" and "You Can Hire Spellers For Minimum Wage".

He was a millionaire, and in one company, held a commission record at the time of slightly over $1-million earned in 37 months. But he could not spell. And flaunted it. He said that, since you could hire perfect spellers for minimum wage, he preferred learning and thinking about more important things, things it was not so easy to pay cheaply for. He was talking about the concept of value. **Value is fundamental.** In boom times or tough times, in big business or small business or any kind of business, even in any occupation or career, the person who makes himself most valuable and creates the most value for others (as they perceive it and are willing to pay for it) always prospers. **If your income isn't where you'd like it to be, you're not creating enough value.** His advice to me, said less elegantly than this, was to find and master something so valuable to enough other people that they will cheerfully pay just about anything for it, and devote *all* your time and energy to selling and doing that. Most people who fail to achieve their aspirations in business do the exact opposite. They let themselves be consumed doing things of low value, then are surprised to discover they reap small harvests. To be fair, getting yourself organized and disciplined to be relentlessly focused on creating value by making yourself more valuable–daily–by always learning more, acquiring and processing more information, running more experiments, making more useful contacts; and by doing the most valuable things you can do is not an easy task. I've written four different books that reveal different paths converging at this same point. Association with others working on this same skill is helpful. Dis-association from those not dedicated to this premise is also helpful.

Which brings me to the other sign. He had zero tolerance for adults still sucking their thumbs. If you wanted to whine and cry like a baby when something didn't go your way, you were told to go home, stick a pacifier in your mouth and hug your blankie. At the time I'm writing this, the economy's a bit tough and bruising and I hear too many adults who sound like babies. Actually, it's just one of those times that the entire economy woke up on the wrong side of the bed grumpy and is telling everybody: thumb-suckers not welcome here. And this must be your personal policy, if you are to prosper and thrive while most others do not. Which is, incidentally, all the time; fewer than 5% have 95% of the wealth flow to them all the time; the disparity is just more stark, the judgment of the critical marketplace more harsh and quick and visible at some times than others. You need zero tolerance for thumb-sucking, personally, or by anybody you permit in your world: staff, associates, vendors, even customers, friends, neighbors, media voices you listen to, authors you read. The power of association is an enormously powerful, irresistible force, for good or evil, for gain or loss, for growth or regression. You dare not discount or underestimate it. You can and should strategically use it for advantage.

The Billionaire's Secrets: OPM, OPR and OPC (You may need them now, more than ever.)

Up in the air. It's a bird, it's a plane—no, it's SuperDan. By the time you read this, I will have flown to four cities and presented my 'no-fail follow-up seminar' and autographed books for four groups in L.A., Chicago, NYC and Orlando. And boy, are my arms tired. At age 20, this might have been fun. It still beats working for a living in a job. But it is annoying every time I hear politicians, particularly a certain presidential candidate, demonizing me for my success and suggesting that the Grand Canyon gap between my high income and others' low incomes is evil and must be narrowed by government theft. In a recent episode of Gene Simmons' show, his daughter ruefully said to him, "I think I'm taking on your work ethic." To which he said, "Good." I'm afraid I'm NOT the kind of Kool-Aid® the no-work-crowd wants to drink. I drive them away from Glazer-Kennedy with this kind of talk. I'm not sorry. And now that an overly generous economy has turned irritable and more demanding, and businesspeople and salespeople are having to dig in and work, I'm hearing a lot of whining. Most salespeople haven't worked in ages. I was comparing notes about this with a friend last week and neither of us could even remember the last time we were "prospected" by a salesperson, followed up on by a salesperson we've previously bought something from. There's crying in the car business, but no salesman or dealer from whom I've purchased new cars in the past 5 years has contacted me. There's mass exodus of real estate agents in surrender, but none I've purchased a property from has contacted me to sell me another. Retail: from the clothing store in my hometown where I spent $1800.00 in my first visit two years ago... from the clothing store in my other home city, where I spent $500.00 on first visit... from a store in Vegas where I spent $2,000.00 on cowboy boots, no salesman has attempted contact. May they all be fired. May they all starve.

Yes, in my WEALTH ATTRACTION book, I write in-depth about liberating yourself from the Work-Money Link. But I never said: don't work, *period.* Nor did I suggest resenting it. I talked about injecting leverage into the equation, as many ways as possible: better customer or client selection; premium prices or fees with higher profit margins; better systems, delegation, outsourcing; smart use of media in place of manual labor; smart time management; money wisely invested. But I never suggested any or all of it as a substitute for work. I presented it as an enhancement of work. It would be more accurate, I suppose, to talk about breaking the strict hours for dollars link.

Leverage. So I want to promote my books. To do my four events in four cities in four consecutive days I used a chartered jet costing over $45,000.00. Sure, I could have flown commercial for a fraction of that cost; if careful and not choosy about routes and time, for as little as $3,000.00. But not done in a four day window. Done this way to minimize consumption of one of my most valuable assets, my time. Besides, I got InfusionSoft to pay for it. When self-made billionaire W. Clement Stone talked about "OPM" – Other Peoples' Money – I listened very carefully. Plus, I tapped into InfusionSoft's lists, and laid the burden of logistics on them. But this also allowed me to tap into Glazer-Kennedy lists and media in a different way, providing Bill with a way to serve Members, promote to non-Members, and support our Independent Business Advisors in four major markets at zero out-of-pocket cost. I created "banked leverage" with current or prospective publisher(s) by doing promotion few other authors could or would do. **I hear you:** "but I'm not an author and not interested in promoting books, so this doesn't apply to me." **You wish I would talk about YOUR business – be it selling insurance or installing draperies or blacksmithing.** But this is the way of all Renegade Millionaires: they're masters at creating time efficient promotion for themselves and their businesses, with someone else picking up the tab. OPM, OPR, and OPC: other peoples' money, other peoples' resources and other peoples' customers. But make no mistake: it's not about avoiding work. In those four days, I will do four days of hard, high pressure, exhausting work. But I'm leveraging it every way I can.

Some Customers Can't Curtail Spending!

IS ANYBODY STILL JUST "THROWING AWAY MONEY" IN THIS ECONOMY? Somewhere between the crash and hasty government rescue of Bear-Stearns and the jobs report showing 80,000 jobs evaporated in one month, a 38 year old trader and real estate investor rounded up a group of his buddies and took them on a "buddy trip" by private helicopter and Hummer limos; to VIP lodging in South Beach; and a game of 'extreme adventure paintball' organized by game-entrepreneurs, all former DEA agents. He isn't as weird as he sounds. In fact, sellers to the rich and super-rich report a "profound EAGERNESS to keep spending" on the part of those hit with investment losses they wish to view as temporary, as a reinforcement of their personal belief system and status – doing so emphasizes their sense of superiority over the masses. The NY Times reported on spending for lavish holiday parties in and around NYC unabated....on a high-end real estate buying boom fueled by discounting: in 07, fewer than 20 Manhattan condos priced above $10-million sold, in 08, over 70 in that price range…and a number of record prices achieved at art auctions this season. And one person's thoughts about money being thrown away are another's idea of justice. In discussing a professionally planned $200,000.00 wedding, a 41-year-old woman marrying a guy she had dated in high school, noted that she was a breast cancer survivor. The travel and entertainment concierge service in Manhattan that arranged the helicopter to South Beach and paintball adventure, In The Know Experiences, reports strong sales still of everything from cigar parties to rentals of racing boats to flights in fighter jets. (Source: NY TIM ES.com)

Managing Your Own Mind

You know the one: if you can keep your head while all about you, others are losing theirs

In uncertain, changing conditions we perceive as threats, it is difficult to maintain any equilibrium, and it is easy to be paralyzed. It's not as simple a matter as optimism vs. pessimism or the old positive thinking v. negative thinking. It's about the quality of your decision-making, the leadership you exhibit to others you influence (staff or clientele), and whether or not you *act* creatively.

The plain truth about panic.

Why does so much panic spread so quickly and easily through so many people whenever tough times occur in a given industry or profession, or the national economy?

Without deep roots, the tree topples in the storm. What are 'deep roots' for the business owner, entrepreneur or sales professional? One, *a system* of selling and conducting business that has proven reliable and profitable, from which he can draw confidence, and which he can stick to with reasoned persistence. If he is advertising and marketing to attract customers, selling to them, retaining and multiplying them absent system, by random and erratic and even impulsive acts, with unplanned and disorganized effort, he'll be blown off course by a stiff breeze.

Two, *a support network* including continuous in-flow of legitimately useful how-to information, coaching by people themselves tested by tough times and proven successful, encouragement and motivation from like-minded, optimistic, forward-thinking businesspeople. Absent this, with no counter-balance to the relentlessly and excessively negative voices of media and peers, he'll bend then break early not late.

Three, *a productive and profitable personal philosophy* sharpened with reading, listening; study of successful achievers; association with the confident and capable, so that he is *conditioned to be opportunistic,* to search for and exploit the opportunities always concealed behind adversity. If he is not daily improving his personal philosophy, he is weakening from the inside out, the core hollow. When Bilbo Baggins said, "I do not like adventures because they make me late for dinner", he expressed profound personal philosophy governing thoughts, actions and outcomes.

When someone says something as simple as "I don't have time to process all that information – I have my business to run", he unwittingly reveals profound personal philosophy as well. You have to investigate your own personal philosophy and evaluate how helpful or unhelpful it is likely to be in weathering storms, in navigating rough seas, in unearthing hidden treasure.

A productive and profitable, personal success philosophy. A sound, organized system. A trustworthy support network. These assets do not develop by accident or luck or randomness. Successful people very deliberately work at developing them, seek to connect to the people and resources and associations most helpful in developing them – and once connected, never risk disconnecting. They strategically assemble these assets in keeping with their own goals, strengths and weaknesses. Key word: strategically.

<u>What Will You Accept?</u>

"He Smashed His Head Bloody Pounding It On His Locker Door - And Broke Off Two Teeth Biting On It."

You may recall a story like that from Dan Jenkins' football novel, *Semi-Tough.* (Made into an okay movie.) The story is reportedly based on actual behavior of Howie Long when he was playing for the Oakland Raiders. You now see a mild-mannered, pleasant Howie on the Sunday morning football show on FOX. That is not the Howie teammates and opponents saw on the field. There, they saw and encountered a man who hated to lose. In his newest novel, about the LPGA, *The Franchise Babe,* Jenkins again talks about the hate-to-lose element.

I find fewer and fewer people exhibiting this. In pro sports. In business. Most are all too willing to accept losing and losses, to shrug them off, to end days without productive accomplishment, to miss sales, to let revenue escape, to let customers disappear, to bank excuses instead of money. And as I said last week, you get what you accept.

I have always <u>hated</u> not doing well. Hate is, or is supposed to be a very strong word. Hate is dark and violent and intense. I mean it that way. I *hate* not doing well. People interfering with my ability to do well, through negligence, incompetence, stupidity, have seen and felt my wrath. Like Howie, I have actually, physically injured myself—smashing fist into wall, steel file cabinet; kicking car fender repeatedly; etc.—in unchecked rage after screwing up badly.

When I set out in the A.M. with a To-Do List, I resist with every fiber of being, carrying an item on it over to the next day. I hate that. When advertising, marketing or sales campaigns are slowed or sabotaged by peoples' sloppy or careless implementation, I immediately begin scheming to rid my life of the culprits. I hate people who don't hate things being f' d up. I approve of the Oriental tradition of falling on one's own sword when performing badly. By normal standards, I suppose I am emotionally unstable or dysfunctional, and might be diagnosed as mentally ill, but then normal standards lead to normal results, which suck. By the way, every doctor always expects me to have high blood pressure. I do not. I *cause* high blood pressure, I don't have it. Seems to me, if you don't care deeply, passionately about getting whatever you're doing right, done fast and on time, done in the way that produces best results, you ought to find something worth caring about to do—or find a way to do nothing at all. If I had a team, I'd much rather have a Howie Long, and have to pry the damaged locker door from his hands and talk him out of the depths of rage, despair and depression over losing, than have a modern-day, laissez-faire, shit happens, we'll try to do better next time wimpus and struggle to talk him into performing. When I look around the ranks of the rich, I see people like me who hate losing. When I look around everywhere else, I see loads of good losers.

At the moment, a lot of willing-to-accept-not-doing-well folks have been handed an extra supply of excuses—gas prices, real estate slump, Lehman Brothers' bankruptcy, etc.—and many are unconsciously delighted to have them. Be careful. *Their* mental illness is contagious.

SELLING IN DIFFICULT CONDITIONS

I say: "Anybody can look good when everybody looks good." The pro deserving admiration—and consistent exceptional reward and security—is the person who fashions himself to do well when most others don't, won't or can't. A lot of quarterbacks can throw the long ball with impressive accuracy in the domed stadiums—so what? Let's see him throw it on a snow and ice flecked field with 20 mile an hour winds. Every so often, an economic cycle separates men from boys, tough from weak, agile from dull. In selling, salespeople often mimic poorly performing athletes when they talk about "being in a slump." And slumps do occur, sometimes with obvious stimulus, such as a recession; other times, solely as a result of private reasons. Either way, it's not the getting into a slump or the existence of slumps that matters. It's how you get yourself to "play your way out."

How To Sell, When People Don't Want To Buy

This may be a new situation for many, brought on by the recession. But I've been selling in this situation, off and on, for a large share of my life – as much as I scheme to avoid it. In my first sales job, I was unwelcome and mostly sold to buyers pre-determined not to even see me and talk to me, let alone buy. I started my business during the Jimmy Carter recession. I have often been on stage selling to audiences comprised of people who left their wallets locked up at home, promised spouses they'd come home without buying anything, or worse, shocked at being sold to at all. I know how to sell when people do not want to buy. The same way you sell under any other circumstances. Selling is selling. And people who can't or won't sell in adverse conditions usually can't or won't sell even when gifted ideal conditions. As Clem Stone said, selling is contingent upon the attitude of the salesperson, not the attitude of the customer.

Actually, people always *want to* buy. At times they may try controlling their buying impulses more than at others; they may have in their heads thoughts of 'can't afford it' or 'better to wait'. But impulse control loses out to white-hot lust every time. Ask Jack Welch, Bill Clinton, Eliot Spitzer, etc., etc. about this. People suspend logic, discipline, pre-conceived ideas, moral beliefs, and anything else required to get what they REALLY want. Barbara Walters apparently desires attention so desperately she has set aside professionalism, pride, good sense, discretion and concern for others to "dish dirt" in her new autobiography; one likely to sell minimally were it not for confessions of her affair with a married, black Congressman and other liaisons. John McCain has garaged his Straight Talk Express because he desperately wants the presidency. People routinely, grossly, outrageously over-pay for particular pieces of real estate, designer shoes, hotel rooms at certain resorts, etc. because they desperately want status and the grudging envy of others. Robert Downey Jr., who considers himself a supremely talented serious actor, puts on a comic book hero costume and then shuffles around the talk show circuit hyping the movie he actually, somewhat obviously views with disdain, because he needs and wants a hit. What people REALLY want governs their behavior most of the time. If you find people reluctant to buy what you are selling, there are only three possible explanations: you're selling to the wrong people; you've failed to connect what you are selling with what they REALLY want; you're a truly inept salesperson. It's NOT 'cuz people aren't buying. They are. Everyday. Non-stop.

Disney's first quarter earnings exceeded their projections and Wall Street expectations, and a major positive contributor was theme park revenues. Why? Shouldn't families be foregoing pricey Disney tickets and vacations at this time? It'll take more than $5 a gallon gas and a wave of foreclosures to stop people from buying what they REALLY want.

How To Get Rich In 'Un-Rich Times'

In the Renegade Millionaire System*, I dispense this advice: #1: BE the Wizard, #2: BEWARE the Wizard. Wizards are very powerful, so it is better to be one than to be influenced by one.

Everybody welcomes the convincing Mystic. *People so **desperately wish** to Believe.* That there is a long lost, ancient or a revolutionary new Something: cure, elixir, formula for easy riches or happy relationships or better sex or children that mind or growing 12 foot high tomato plants; a gizmo that turns corn into fuel or tree bark into gold doubloons; an Answer Man, Seer, Keeper of Secrets. And in dark times, this desire intensifies. In dark times even kings subjugate themselves to the Mystics—which you know if you've studied history. People really don't want rational explanations for how you do what you do, they prefer Believing that you possess Mystical Powers and Magical Secrets that you will use for their benefit. To underestimate the power of secrets and secret powers is to ignore how humanity has been manipulated, controlled and ruled since its beginnings.

In these times, you can rise to greater heights of influence and power than at any other time, by turning up the wattage on your mysticism. In the dark, you glow. Doesn't matter if you dispense investment advice or lawn care advice, are a dog whisperer or a presidential candidate, or a tax attorney or a mattress manufacturer—now, more than ever, is the time to speak of secret techniques and magic ingredients and unique abilities. To offer absolute certainty in an uncertain world. To declare unique and profound importance.

I'm speaking now about how you present yourself to the world.

If you sell a particular kind of mattress, you must present it as THE—emphasis on key word: THE—first, best, only "magic", based on top secret technology invented for NASA and Olympic athletes—that relieves all back pain, delivers 10,000 more REM's per night, lets cellular structure rejuvenate thus slowing aging, helps you lose weight while you sleep; is THE secret to eternal youth and vitality. It must be THE GREATEST discovery in medical science of this century. And you, as its spokesperson, must be the Grand Mystic of Sleep Science. You need an arsenal of Amazing Facts at your disposal. You need practiced language and Profound Statements. You must convincingly promise THE Cure. For whatever ails them, economically, emotionally, physically. To advance your education, I strongly suggest getting and reading the book *CHARLATAN*. It reads like a novel but is non-fiction. Not that you should be a charlatan; I presume you deliver legitimate value in whatever you sell or do. But that you should use the techniques of the master-charlatans of the ages. Nothing less will do.

When a group becomes lost and frightened in a dark cave, the man with the only flashlight automatically becomes their leader. Key word: only. It's time to present yourself as the person with THE ONLY flashlight.

Now Is The Time To Do It Differently
"Help! - I Can't Get Out Of The Box I Put Myself In!"

The fast food industry got the idea for drive-in windows *from banks.* I guess there was a McDonald's executive sitting at the bank drive-through one day who thought, "I don't think we can fit the milkshakes in these tubes, but..." Netjets, the leader in fractional jet ownership, now owned by Warren Buffet, owes its birth to the vacation time-share industry. The microwave in your kitchen was not originally intended to go there; its original manufacturer, Litton, believed no consumer would buy it and built them only for restaurants. When was the last time you heard of Litton? What does this tell you? That successful businesses live or die by cross-industry 'borrowing' of ideas, that inspiration more often comes from outside the box than from within. Ordinary businesses stay ordinary, their owners eking out only ordinary incomes—and working too hard for them—as long as those owners foolishly and stubbornly, mentally stay in their own tiny backyard. Breakthroughs come from bringing fresh ideas found outside one's own business in and applying them in new ways. **You choose to limit or expand your income** by the way you reject or embrace ideas found far afield from your present modus operandi and industry norms.

The vast majority of ordinary businesspeople with ordinary incomes and never-ending ordinary complaints about how hard they work but how little they gain, about being unable to compete with the bigger and cheaper...have this in common: they get their hands on powerful information like that in this very publication and waste their time and energy in the *non*-creative activity of finding all the ways it *can't* and *doesn't* apply to them. Some people have such teeny, tiny, calcified, crippled imaginations they can only appreciate an example precisely matched to them—*oh, that won't work for me because her place sells pizza and I sell Chinese food, and hers is in a medium sized city and I'm in a small town, and it rains a lot where she is but it's sunny here; you have to show me an example from a Chinese restaurant in a small town where it's hot and dry.* Fools stay stuck in the very limiting "But My Business Is Different" box, thereby negating the value of 99% of every successful strategy, example, model they see or are presented with.

My client list is, fortunately, chock full of people who think in very opposite ways. They get rich by finding the *non*-obvious opportunities. Living creatively. Adapting tried-and-true winning strategies from somewhere else to where they are. They attack each issue of my newsletter, each book I suggest to them, with yellow hi-liter and bias for action, not closed mind. They are willing, even eager to "re-imagine" their businesses while others have Bilbo Baggins' (The Hobbit) attitude: not interested in *adventures*—they make you late for dinner.

One of the most successful marketing strategies of all time is called 'gift with appointment.' Today, it brings new patients into dentists' offices, affluent investors to financial advisors' seminars, new home buyers to developments and resort communities, and is in play in hundreds of fields, helping to create millions of sales appointments every week. To the best of my knowledge, it came from a woman named Estee Lauder. I wonder how many people from how many different fields ignored it for how long, because: "Nothing having to do with selling lipsticks and perfumes could possibly apply to MY business. MY business is different."

"BATTEN DOWN THE HATCHES"

In stormy economic seas, investors turn more attention to PRESERVATION of capital vs. growth or yield; business owners must give more attention to PRESERVATION of their business' equity – which actually lies almost entirely in their customers and their relationship with their customers, and their personal capital i.e. their time and energy. Regrettably, many do not pay nearly enough attention to these things until forced to, by adverse circumstances.

The Price of Negligence

In my relentless search for I don't know what, I found an article in the December 1, 2008 edition of Nation's Restaurant News, the trade journal of the restaurant industry, headlined: "Operators Bank On Profit And Loss Scrutiny To Stay Afloat." It made me laugh out loud. The article states that "maximizing the profit and loss statement has become a mantra for restaurant operators *during the current economic downturn.*" This is then presented as some sort of horrific torture imposed on the owners by a vicious economy. What is *not* said, but should be, is that maximizing profit shouldn't be paid attention to only after dire economic conditions occur, to be given temporary priority, only until 'things get better.' **It's supposed to be what anybody responsible for operating a business does everyday.** Including what's then described in the article: ferreting out and cutting wasteful spending, controlling labor and administrative costs; creating products, offers and price propositions customers really want. Any business owner complaining about having to attend to these priorities because of a recession is a moron, and any trade-journal writer taking them seriously is dumber than a sandbox.

But *this* is why so many businesses fail. When you turn on the news to see insurance giants exposed as valueless houses of cards, venerable auto companies as manufacturers of nothing but debt, retail and restaurant chains announcing massive store closings, make no mistake: their managements can point their fingers at the recession all they like, but it's a lie. All the tough economy has done is expose the failures of the people at the helms. Businesses never fail. People fail to run them profitably. Much of that is pure and simple negligence. To be clear, negligence is, by definition, the failure to act with the care a prudent person would exercise.

So, when Mort Zuckerman loses 30-million or 300-million of his charity's dollars by having it all invested with Bernie Madoff for three years, claiming he didn't even know the money was invested there by somebody he delegated its management to, he is obviously negligent. If you leave a rake pointy side up on your front porch steps, with the lights burnt out, and the pizza delivery guy steps on it and falls and breaks his leg, you are negligent, will be successfully sued, and see your insurance rates go up. There is a price for negligence, and there's supposed to be. In business, failure to closely and constantly monitor all the important numbers and benchmarks and predictive indicators (as detailed in Chapter 43 of my book *'No B. S. Ruthless Management of People and Profits')* is negligence of the highest order. Its bill may go unnoticed in boom times when money flows easily and everyone does well, but when the warm breezes change to bitter cold wind, and the accumulated tab for such negligence is presented and payment demanded, much pain occurs, much hand-wringing and whining and crying about the mean 'n nasty recession is heard, and fools commiserate with each other, sharing the misery of their own sins of negligence.

If you own a business, by gum, run the darned thing. Maximize profits every way you can, and never stop trying to find new and better ways to do so, from every valid source of input, ideas and information you can get your hands on or get connected with. At day's end, ask: what do I know now (about maximizing profits) that I didn't know this morning? And: what am I going to do tomorrow as a result of what I've learned?

Anything less is negligence.

How To Make A Lot More Money, Fast

Odds are, your business lost a lot of customers last year. There are holes in your bucket. And odds are, you can't say for sure how many you lost, who you lost, why you lost them or where they went and are now. If you do nothing different, I can send you this same fax next year too. **A great way to make more money is to stop losing customers, beginning with the next one you are about to lose.**

This will require accurately determining what a customer is worth and what cost of replacing a customer really is...so you can decide how much you are willing to invest NOT to lose a customer.

Next, taking that investment and deciding how to apportion it, between preventive measures and rescue and recovery measures. Then designing or re-designing, beefing up and actually implementing both, the "keep 'em" program and the "rescue/recovery" program. Then testing, evaluating, improving, again and again.

In the aforementioned "Dan and Bill's Strategy Day", we spent a lot of time – and now Bill will spend a lot of time, money and work – doing exactly this, and we already have low loss/high retention stats and sophisticated, multi-step, multi-faceted "stick" (for new); "keep" (for continuing), and "rescue and recovery" (for lost) programs. (Do *you?).* But now we will add to, experiment with, refine and hopefully improve all three. (Will *you?)* I counted 23 different, specific "adjustments" we agreed on, all to be implemented within the next 90 days; some minor, some major, some simple, some painfully complex. (How many improvements are *you* testing in *your* three programs by April 30?)

Every year, I'm somebody's lost customer. Many don't even realize I'm lost. I guess they think "gee, he hasn't been in, in a while", if they think at all. Every year, national companies and local shops lose me as a customer. I can't recall even one, ever, doing anything proactive and significant about their loss.

Okay, so that's one very practical suggestion for making a lot more money fast. Here's another: upgrade customers before you lose 'em. You'll then lose less automatically. You ought to give that a lot of thought.

You ought to HATE—and I mean, *HATE*—losing customers. The athletes or teams who win a lot hate losing —even more than they like winning. To win races, you've got to hate losing. Winning is not sufficient motivation. You NEED to understand the true economics of losing customers. You NEED to get yourself highly motivated and passionately committed to invest aggressively in not losing customers. By the way, any nitwit can get customers. Thousands of dot-com nitwits got 'em by the millions with no business model at all. No genius in getting them. But no successful business exists based on its owners' ability to get customers. Successful businesses sustain themselves only by keeping them.

Race Your Best Horse A Lot

The other day, I was talking with Diana Nightingale, the late Earl Nightingale's wife, co-author and business partner. Earl, you hopefully recall, recorded 'The Strangest Secret', and was, in his time, the most famous voice of personal development. I have so frequently referenced the two life-making, fortune-making ideas I got from Earl that I won't re-state them here. Anyway, Diana said that basically Earl was a 'one note', in that he had one, relatively simple idea at core of literally tens of thousands of hours of radio broadcasts, lectures, recorded courses as well as a warehouse of written material; the strangest secret, that we become what we think about most—and that we have total control over that choice. That we are product of our own (choices of) thought was not original with Earl, but he made it his own, and made himself prominent, popular and wealthy riding just that horse.

I have two different speeches that each made me millions of dollars, one over several years, one over ten years, without change. I did not get up in the morning tinkering with them or searching for a newer, shinier, maybe better one; I got up looking for more opportunities and the best opportunities to use them.

Too many people spend too much time "flitting." Their best racehorse stands in the stall without getting proper exercise or even missing a week of racing while they attend an auction looking for a *new* horse. Clients sometimes show me ten different things they're working on, while one proven winner is used to only a fraction of its capacity. My advice is often: mail more of *that.* Let's not even discuss the others. Let's talk about mailing more of *that.* I have one client who is poster boy for such ADD. His attention span teeny, appetite huge, energy woefully diffused, so every achievement is accompanied by a lot of sewage in its wake from incomplete and insufficient attention to detail and follow-through. In simple terms, this the constant re-creating of the web site when what is really needed is more traffic to it and more disciplined, diligent follow-up of the leads it produces.

There are two divided schools of thought on this, both wrong. One: if it ain't broke, don't fix it. As Mike Vance accurately asserts, with that philosophy, we'd be reading by candlelight and riding to work every morning with big pooper-scooper by our side. Two: if it ain't broke, break it. This is kaizen on steroids; constant improvement by constant revolution, never just evolution. But this defies one of the greatest of all business objectives; the ownership of the most valuable of assets; an *evergreen* product, service, ad, sales letter, marketing system that reliably puts predictable sums into your bank account at a sure and steady pace. The few clients I have with the discipline to do it love owning the direct-mail campaign that never fails, that never wears out, that need not be touched or altered for years and years. As usual, no single approach is right or sufficient. Business is more complex than that. And, incidentally, Diana's both right and wrong in her summation of Earl's work. She's right in that everything was a re-statement of a single idea, but still, almost every re-statement was wrapped in different context, itself presenting littler but still significant nuances on the theme, mini-ideas, and applications. Not even a single sentence can really be about just a single idea unless read by a simpleminded person.

This excerpt is reprinted from Chapter 17 of "**No B.S. Business Success**" by Dan Kennedy.

HOW TO GET A BUSINESS OUT OF TROUBLE

One ought never to turn one's back on a threatened danger and try to run away from it. If you do that, you will double the danger. But if you meet it promptly and without flinching, you will reduce it by half. Never run away from anything. Never.

- Winston Churchill

Hopefully you'll never need the advice in this brief chapter. Hopefully.

I have been involved in a couple of business turnarounds and helped clients with others. I've also made a point of studying some of the best-known, big-name turnaround experts, and I can tell you that there is very little difference between getting one business or another out of trouble. Your options for action are rather limited.

The very first, crucial step is honesty. You've got to forget all about protecting your ego and blaming others. None of that matters when the kettle is boiling over. You have to diagnose and identify problems, period. You need all the gory details. No one can be allowed to hide anything; no one can be allowed to feel they have to hide anything.

This is very tough to achieve. Everybody's natural responses are to cover their own tracks as best they can. If people can't or won't be honest with themselves and each other about the problems, either the people have to go, fast, or the business goes under. That's it.

AS LONG AS THERE'S A PULSE, THERE'S HOPE

The only absolutely certain death blow for a troubled business is running out of cash. There's little else that's irreversible.

Poisoned Tylenol killed people but the business survived. Auto makers routinely recall thousands of cars with potentially lethal defects but they survive. Key people quit, big competitors move in, fires and floods happen, but businesses survive. I don't think there's any business problem that can't be beat as long as there's cash flow. During a turnaround period, profit and loss is even irrelevant. But cash flow is everything.

I've run a company completely out of cash on two occasions. Miraculously, this company got through both these situations. On one of those occasions, the company took five weeks to recover from a $47,000.00 checking account overdraft. I spent those five weeks walking around with just the few crinkled dollar bills in my pocket, coasting downhill in my car to conserve gas, jumping out of my skin at every phone call, just waiting for the final death nudge to come from somewhere. I've faced cash-flow problems since, but I learned my lesson. No matter the pressure, I will not take a business down to zero cash.

If you find your business in a cash-flow crunch, you must immediately become very tight-fisted about parting with each penny. Pay bills in tiny pieces. Trickle it out. Negotiate new terms with vendors as fast as you can. Sacrifice some vendors if you must. Put tiny dabs of grease on the squeakiest wheels. But never, never spend down to zero or, worse, below zero, to appease the wolves. Let them stand out their baying and scratching at the door, but keep the few spare bullets in your gun at all times.

FORGET "KINDER AND GENTLER"

Cut costs with the ax, not a surgical knife. If there's any turnaround mistake I've made more than once, it's being too gentle and conservative in the cutting. You can always put a person or function back in if you must. To start getting out of trouble, though, swing your ax in a wide arc. Cut everywhere. Spare no one, no thing. Cut, cut, cut.

In one turnaround situation, I let 38 people go in one day. I had more blood on my hands than the monster in a cheap horror movie. It was really awful. One of the top people asked me: "How do you know you can function without some of these people?" I said: "I don't." I really didn't. I didn't have time to sort out who was really important and who wasn't. I had to stop the cash hemorrhage first, to even get a minute to think. So I swung the ax with abandon. And I'd do it again without a second thought if presented with a similar situation.

PULL TOGETHER A PLAN

Once you've done what you can to stop the cash from pouring out of the business' wounds, bring everything to a near stop for a few days, get the best brains together you can, lock yourselves up in a quiet room without interruptions, and pull together a plan.

Without a plan, you'll make the mistake I made in the first turnaround crisis I dealt with. I started out by instantly reacting to each and every new problem that reared its ugly head, each howling wolf as it appeared at the door. I'd drop one thing to face the other, then turn from that to the next noise in the dark. Pretty soon I was spinning around like a top. One night, long after everybody else had left, I was in my chair behind my desk, sweaty, bone tired, exhausted. I realized I was completely out of control.

Dan Kennedy's Eternal Truth #21
When you're up to your neck in alligators,
it's difficult to remember that your original
objective was to drain the swamp.

Then I shut the door and put together a believable, step-by-step business plan with a lot of details for the first six months and more general ideas for the next six. With this battle plan in hand, I had confidence; I had the ability to engineer cooperation from others. Then I placed a limit on the amount of time each day dedicated to problems. When we hit the quota for the day, that was it; the rest of the problems had to stand in line until the next day. Each day, I set aside a certain amount of time to implement the business plan. With plan in hand, I restored order and kept myself out of the padded room.

DON'T HIDE

If your business owes a lot of money to a lot of creditors, you'll be tempted to hide. Big mistake. You or someone you give this responsibility to must keep the lines of communication open for those creditors and be as truthful as possible with them. When you can't promise a payment amount and date, don't; promise what you can, even if that's only the date and time you'll next communicate.

Target the creditors hurting your cash flow most for comprehensive renegotiation. Take your new business plan and meet in person if possible. At the least, phone or fax them, and shoot for the very best deal you can get.

For example, let's say you owe XYZ Company $20,000.00, all past due. You might get that $20,000.00 switched from a trade payable to a long-term, five-year installment note, interest only for the first year, and agree on new purchases to pay one-third with order, one-third on delivery, and one-third in 30 days. This takes $20,000.00 out of your current struggle altogether. Otherwise, you'd be whacking away at that $500.00 or $1,000.00 at a time, the creditor would never be happy, and getting needed goods would probably be next to impossible.

Facing trouble head-on, more often than not, earns respect and promotes cooperation.

DON'T TAKE IT PERSONALLY

Okay, your business is in trouble and you were captain of the ship while it smashed into the rocks. That's bad. But everybody makes mistakes. You're not the first, you won't be the last, and there is no shame in screwing up. The only cause for shame would be giving up without a fight. If you are genuinely trying to do the best you can, there's nothing to be ashamed of.

Beating yourself up or letting somebody else beat you up as a person is uncalled for and, obviously, unproductive. You have to be able to step out of the emotion and be a tough-minded turnaround consultant for your own business.

DIRECT YOUR ENERGY TO BUSINESS RENOVATION

Even if it's only an hour, grab a certain amount of time each and every day and go to work on reinventing your business. Get to the very core of the problems. During a turnaround, you'll be doing a lot of patching work, and that's okay, but while you're patching up cuts and bruises you need to be the visionary designer of a whole new and improved operation.

Don G. had a chain of six restaurants that wound up in deep trouble. While he did all the things we've been talking about with the entire chain, he also took just one of the locations as his "new" model, and made major changes there, literally inventing a new and different restaurant operation, from A to Z. After a year, the entire company had limped its way back into positive cash flow, largely through debt restructuring and cost-cutting, and although the entire business was still operating at a net loss, the new model was consistently hitting a 30% profit mark. Don now had a model to duplicate in his other five locations, which allowed him to again restructure debt, get some new investment capital, quickly make over the other five locations, and by the end of the second year of the turnaround, chalk up several hundred thousand dollars in profit.

At this point, the local beer distributor who supplied his restaurants bought into his company, contributed enough capital to wipe out all the high-interest debt, and open four more locations. Three years later, they sold the entire business to a national food-service company and walked away millionaires.

If Don had waited until he had his entire turnaround process implemented to go to work on his core business's reinvention, all these good things would not have happened, and he might have run out of time and money before ever getting to try his new plan.

Create your own 5-Point Recession Rescue Plan...by selecting key ideas from everything you've just read and converting them to action strategies. A few examples are included here to get you started...

"THE PLAN"

1. STRENGTHEN YOUR PRESENT BUSINESS

Three ways I can increase the value offered to my customers/ prospects:

____

____

____

Three (additional) ways I can prevent losses of customers or rescue inactives:

____

____

____

How can I more "tightly" manage my business?—daily benchmarks and measurements:

____

____

____

A thorough review of my SYSTEM, from first point of contact between a potential customer and my business through to first sale and post-sale reveals gaps and holes, and these opportunities to improve:

____

____

____

2. FIND A NEW SOURCE OF CUSTOMERS/ CLIENTS TO MATCH YOUR BUSINESS TO:

WHO—*precisely*—can I be of greatest, clearest value to now?

____

____

____

How can I access **OPC**—Other People's Customers?
How can OPC lead me to the ideal 'Who's' identified above?

____

____

____

What **boundaries** am I operating within, that can be expanded or erased?

____

____

____

3. Launch Multiple Initiatives

EXTERNAL—TO GET NEW CUSTOMERS

To access OPC, pursue new strategic alliances, parasite-host relationships, joint venture or co-op promotion opportunities with as many business owners and owners of lists as possible… simultaneously!

____

____

____

INTERNAL—TO SELL MORE/TO OPERATE MORE PROFITABLY

____

____

____

4. WORK ON YOUR OWN THINKING AND THAT OF THOSE YOU NEED TO INFLUENCE

Focus on what you can control. INSIST on productivity and progress EVERY day and accept no excuses. **Things I Can Do EVERY Day To Improve Business:**

____

____

____

5. ACT AGRESSIVELY (NOT RECKLESSLY, BUT AGGRESSIVELY)

Re-position and present yourself as THE expert with THE solution to your customers' needs/desires… THE person in possession of THE ONLY flashlight in the darkness. 3 Ways to build your Status:

____

____

____

For more assistance with a complete Plan, consult the book, THE ULTIMATE MARKETING PLAN.

About the Author

John S. Cohoat is an entrepreneur and Independent Business Advisor for the Northern Indiana/Southwest Michigan Chapter of Glazer-Kennedy Insider's Circle. He has owned several small businesses including an ice cream manufacturer, restaurants, a golf training business and a country inn. He refers to himself a "recovering CPA" and is a former hospital Chief Executive Officer, also holding several other healthcare executive positions. He provides coaching, education, consulting and copywriting for small businesses, professionals in private practice and entrepreneurs. More information is available at www.cohoatbusinessgrowth.com.

A native Hoosier, John graduated from the University of Notre Dame and received an MBA from the University of Pittsburgh. He lives in Middlebury, Indiana with his wife Adrienne and has five children.

Acknowledgements

First, I'd like to mention the executives of the ten businesses featured in this book. They are truly the "stars of the show". Of all the companies I had considered for the book, only one chose not to be included. The leaders interviewed were quite willing to share their time, information about their companies and their opinions freely with me. My thanks to them for allowing me to tell their stories.

Thanks also to Dan Kennedy. For those of you who don't know him, suffice it to say that he has inspired thousands of entrepreneurs and has a way of approaching business and marketing that is truly unique. To have him lend his endorsement to my book and allow me to include a chapter of his thoughts is something I cannot repay. Know that I appreciate what an honor it is to have Dan associated with my efforts to get this story out.

Thanks also to my wife Adrienne, my brother Matt and my son John T. Cohoat for reviewing early drafts of the book and providing great feedback and good ideas. My mom, Mary, has been on me since I was young to write a book and when I told her about this one, she was thrilled. I'm happy that she will be able to enjoy it in her own way.

Finally, I have to mention that much of the inspiration for the original concept for the book came when I wondered how my father, John J. Cohoat and my father-in-law Donald W. Berg would have reacted to the events of late 2008 and 2009. Both served in the military and have passed on. My thinking is that their service was not to support the ways our leaders have taken us the last several years. This book is an attempt to get us back on the path they would have espoused and to repudiate a mentality and set of policies that will certainly lead to destruction of all they stood for. They loved their Country and would not have been pleased with what we are experiencing now.

Special Opportunity for Readers of No Thank You, Mr. President:

The Most Incredible FREE Gift Ever

($613.91 Worth of Pure Moneymaking Information)

Dan Kennedy & Bill Glazer are offering an incredible opportunity for you to see WHY Glazer-Kennedy Insider's Circle™ is known as "THE PLACE" where entrepreneurs seeking FAST and Dramatic Growth and greater Control, Independence, and Security come together. Dan & Bill want to give you **$613.91 worth of pure Money-Making Information** including TWO months as an 'Elite' Gold Member of Glazer-Kennedy's Insider's Circle™. You'll receive a steady stream of MILLIONAIRE Maker Information including:

* Glazer-Kennedy University: Series of 3 Webinars (Value = $387.00)

The 10 "BIG Breakthroughs in Business Life *with Dan Kennedy*

- HOW Any Entrepreneur or Sales Professional can Multiply INCOME by 10X
- **HOW to Avoid Once and for All being an *"Advertising Victim"***
- The "*Hidden Goldmine*" in Everyone's Business and HOW to Capitalize on it
- **The BIGGEST MISTAKE most Entrepreneurs make in their Marketing**
- And the BIGGEEE…Getting Customers Seeking You Out.

The ESSENTIALS to Writing Million Dollar Ads & Sales Letters BOTH Online & Offline *with Marketing & Advertising Coach, Bill Glazer*

- How to INCREASE the Selling Power of All Your Advertising by Learning the 13 "Must Have" Direct Response Principles
- **Key Elements that Determine the Success of Your Website**
- HOW to Craft a Headline the Grabs the Reader's Attention
- **How to Create an Irresistible Offer that Melts Away Any Resistance to Buy**
- The Best Ways to Create Urgency and Inspire IMMEDIATE Response
- ***"Insider Strategies"* to INCREASE Response that you Must be using both ONLINE & Offline**

The ESSENTIALS of Productivity & Implementation for Entrepreneurs *w/ Peak Performance Coach Lee Milteer*

- How to Almost INSTANTLY be MORE Effective, Creative, Profitable, and Take MORE Time Off
- **HOW to Master the "Inner Game" of Personal Peak Productivity**
- How to Get MORE Done in Less Time
- **HOW to Get Others to Work On Your Schedule**
- How to Create Clear Goals for SUCESSFUL Implementation
- And Finally the BIGGEE…How to Stop Talking and Planning Your Dreams and Start Implementing Them into Reality

*'Elite' Gold Insider's Circle Membership (Two Month Value = $99.94):

- Two Issues of ***The No B.S.® Marketing Letter:***

Each issue is at least 12 pages—usually MORE—Overflowing with **the latest Marketing & Moneymaking Strategies.** Current members refer to it as a day-long intense seminar in print, arriving by first class mail every month. There are ALWAYS terrific examples of ***"What's-Working-NOW"* Strategies**, timely Marketing news, trends, ongoing teaching of Dan Kennedy's Most IMPORTANT Strategies … and MORE. As soon as it arrives in your mailbox you'll want to find a quiet place, grab a highlighter, and devour every word.

- Two CDs Of The **EXCLUSIVE GOLD AUDIO INTERVIEWS**

These are EXCLUSIVE interviews with successful users of direct response advertising, leading experts and entrepreneurs in direct marketing, and famous business authors and speakers. Use them to turn commuting hours into "POWER Thinking" hours.

*The New Member No B.S.® Income Explosion Guide & CD (Value = $29.97)

This resource is especially designed for NEW MEMBERS to show them HOW they can join the thousands of Established Members **creating exciting sales and PROFIT growth** in their Business, Practices, or Sales Careers & Greater SUCCESS in their Business lives.

Income Explosion FAST START Tele-Seminar with Dan Kennedy, Bill Glazer, and Lee Milteer (Value = $97.00)

Attend from the privacy and comfort of your home or office ... hear a DYNAMIC discussion of Key Advertising, Marketing, Promotion, Entrepreneurial & Phenomenon strategies, PLUS answers to the most Frequently Asked Questions about these Strategies

*You'll also get these Exclusive "Members Only" Perks:

- **Special FREE Gold Member CALL-IN TIMES:** Several times a year, Dan & I schedule Gold-Member ONLY Call-In times
- **Gold Member RESTRICTED ACCESS WEBSITE**: Past issues of the ***No B.S.® Marketing Letter***, articles, special news, etc.
- **Continually Updated MILLION DOLLAR RESOURCE DIRECTORY** with Contacts and Resources Dan & his clients use.

To activate your MOST INCREDIBLE FREE GIFT EVER you only pay a one-time charge of $19.95 (or $39.95 for Int'l subscribers) to cover postage (this is for everything). **After your 2-Month FREE test-drive, you will automatically continue at the lowest Gold Member price of $59.97 per month. Should you decide to cancel your membership, you can do so at any time by calling Glazer-Kennedy Insider's Circle™ at 410-825-8600 or faxing a cancellation note to 410-825-3301 (Monday through Friday 9am–5pm). Remember, your credit card will NOT be charged the low monthly membership fee until the beginning of the 3rd month, which means you will receive 2 full issues to read, test, and** profit from all of the powerful techniques and strategies you get from being an Insider's Circle Gold Member. **And of course, it's impossible for you to lose, because if you don't absolutely LOVE everything you get, you can simply cancel your membership before the third month and never get billed a single penny for membership.**

EMAIL REQUIRED IN ORDER TO NOTIFY YOU ABOUT THE GLAZER-KENNEDY UNIVERSITY WEBINARS AND FAST START TELESEMINAR

Name ______________________ Business Name ______________________

Address ____

City ______________ State _____ Zip _______ e-mail* ______________

Phone ______________________ Fax______________________

Credit Card Instructions to Cover $19.95 for Shipping & Handling:

____Visa ____MasterCard ____ American Express ____ Discover

Credit Card Number ______________________ Exp. Date ____________

Signature ______________________ Date ____________

Providing this information constitutes your permission for Glazer-Kennedy Insider's Circle™ to contact you regarding related information via mail, e-mail, fax, and phone.

Special Opportunity for Readers of "No Thank You, Mr. President"
FAX Back To: 410-825-3301 or visit www.cohoatbusinessgrowth.com and click on Most Incredible Gift Ever Or Mail to: 401 Jefferson Ave, Towson, MD 21286

BUY A SHARE OF THE FUTURE IN YOUR COMMUNITY

These certificates make great holiday, graduation and birthday gifts that can be personalized with the recipient's name. The cost of one S.H.A.R.E. or one square foot is $54.17. The personalized certificate is suitable for framing and will state the number of shares purchased and the amount of each share, as well as the recipient's name. The home that you participate in "building" will last for many years and will continue to grow in value.

Here is a sample SHARE certificate:

YES, I WOULD LIKE TO HELP!

I support the work that Habitat for Humanity does and I want to be part of the excitement! As a donor, I will receive periodic updates on your construction activities but, more importantly, I know my gift will help a family in our community realize the dream of homeownership. ***I would like to SHARE in your efforts against substandard housing in my community!*** *(Please print below)*

PLEASE SEND ME ___________ SHARES at $54.17 EACH = $ $____________

In Honor Of: ____

Occasion: *(Circle One)* *HOLIDAY* *BIRTHDAY* *ANNIVERSARY*

OTHER: ____

Address of Recipient: ______________________________________

Gift From: ________________ ***Donor Address:*** ________________

Donor Email: ____

I AM ENCLOSING A CHECK FOR $ $____________ PAYABLE TO HABITAT FOR HUMANITY OR PLEASE CHARGE MY VISA OR MASTERCARD *(CIRCLE ONE)*

Card Number ______________________________ Expiration Date: ____________

Name as it appears on Credit Card ________________ Charge Amount $ __________

Signature ____

Billing Address ____

Telephone # Day ________________________ Eve ________________________

PLEASE NOTE: Your contribution is tax-deductible to the fullest extent allowed by law.

Habitat for Humanity • P.O. Box 1443 • Newport News, VA 23601 • 757-596-5553

www.HelpHabitatforHumanity.org

LaVergne, TN USA
28 May 2010
184359LV00001B/1/P